A clarion call to "lead with purpose," _Cadence of Care offers a wise_ and practical guide for deepening and enriching client relationships. Owings discusses the importance of our stories and those of our clients, reminds us of the power of focused listening and suggests proven ways to respond to ten types of loss. A compelling exposition of the humanity which lies at the heart of the advisory enterprise, this book will improve and ennoble anyone's practice.

Robert B. Seaberg, Ph.D.
Intersect Consulting, LLC

Tim Owings understands what all the great ones know. People who trust you are far more important than all the product knowledge in the world.

Don Connelly
Don Connelly Associates

Once again, Tim Owings has taken the words of the English language and the incredible heart of a servant and blended them together to create a presence in someone's life while managing the business side with care and compassion. _Cadence of Care_ captures the stunning roadmap of caring for clients from the financial element to the emotional realities that create a lifetime partnership. Right on target!

Charlene P. Sizemore, President
Workforce Capital, LLC

Should financial advisors have the same relationship with their clients as clergy have with their parishioners? The answer is "yes!" The concepts Tim Owings shares in his book provide a comprehensive blueprint to integrate into practice that same level of pastoral care and compassion. Helping someone achieve financial stability at various stages in life requires not only a knowledge of risk tolerance and rates of return but also a focused understanding of an individual's needs and vulnerabilities. I believe the insights gleaned from *Cadence of Care* will instill in financial advisors a greater sense of awareness in meeting the goals and aspirations of their clients.

Marc D. Miller, Ph.D.
Dean of the School of Business
Henderson State University

It is very rare when I discover that a multi-talented friend is also an excellent writer. Such is the case with Tim Owings. On almost every page of this book, there is a brilliant insight. So many "take-aways". Not to be missed.

Major General Perry M. Smith (Ret.)
Author, *Rules and Tools for Leaders*

Tim Owings' wisdom and compassion jump off the page in his powerful book, *Cadence of Care*. In a rigorous, entertaining manner, he leads us through the labyrinth of relationships accompanying the complex role of being a trusted advisor. In my thirty years of close friendship with him, I have come to know him well. He is loyal in the crunch times, virtuoso with words and music, empathetic in the tragic times, and trustworthy every single day. All of that and more is presented in this volume, amplified by the most remarkable "to do" lists for being your best. Read it and take notes—you will be glad you did!

Bill Curry

We often attempt to separate events into categories when our interpersonal worlds collide. The reality is, we experience life holistically: mind, body, and spirit. Tim Owings does a masterful job demonstrating the need for understanding human relationships and applying those principles to business and life. *Cadence of Care* serves as a guide for the journey, filled with practical suggestions and moving illustrations. It is a must read for anyone who serves as an advisor to others.

Jeffrey Flowers, D.Min.
Director of Pastoral Care and Counseling
Augusta University Health System

Real success and lasting relationships come from the personal care and attention one brings to clients. In *Cadence of Care*, Tim Owings creatively reminds us that whether managing assets or navigating the legal system, trust begins, grows, and deepens from caring relationships.

Wyck Knox
Kilpatrick Townsend & Stockton, LLP

ЈЬ

Stroud & Hall Publishers
P.O. Box 27210
Macon, Ga 31221
www.stroudhall.com

©2016 TL Owings & Associates, LLC

The paper used in this publication meets the minimum requirements
of American National Standard for Information Sciences—
Permanence of Paper for Printed Library Materials.
ANSI Z39.48–1984. (alk. paper)

Library of Congress Cataloging-in-Publication Data

Names: Owings, Timothy, author.
Title: Cadence of care : imagining a transformed advisor-client experience /
  by Tim Owings.
Description: Macon, GA : Stroud & Hall Publishing, [2016] I Includes
  bibliographical references
Identifiers: LCCN 2016040611 I ISBN 9780989337373 (pbk. : alk. paper)
Subjects: LCSH: Investment advisor-client relationships. I Investment
  advisors.
Classification: LCC HG4621 .O94 2016 I DDC 332.6/2--dc23
LC record available at https://lccn.loc.gov/2016040611

CADENCE

of CARE

IMAGINING A TRANSFORMED
ADVISOR-CLIENT EXPERIENCE

Tim Owings, Ph.D., CFP®

FOREWORD BY BOB DOLL

Contents

Foreword

What does it mean for a financial advisor to *care* for a client? Why should you put their interests first, and help them manage risk as they strive to meet financial goals? Why should you care? In *Cadence of Care*, Tim Owings asserts that the rhythm of practice management must change if you want your relationships to deepen and your business to grow. While most applicable to financial advisors, the tools, techniques and principles in this book will also resonate with attorneys, CPAs, bankers, human resource directors, and others.

Today, as robo-advisors are increasingly commonplace, the added dimension of "the personal touch" becomes even more critical. Confronted with the proliferation of choice, social media, and the ease of moving from one company and advisor to another, customer satisfaction is ever more critical. Technical training is entry stakes. More subtle, yet rising in importance is the art of relationships that complement the core competency of any profession. It is becoming critical for professionals to service clients with a golden glove. Your customers are navigating a new terrain. Likewise, advisors are circumnavigating the complexities of marriage and divorce, multiple jobs and careers, heightened mobility, increased longevity and an ever-expanding definition of what it means to be retired. Knowing, caring for, and dare I use the word, loving your clients elevates the relationship and the probability of excellent outcomes.

All too often, client care and customer service is reactive—arriving after a disruption, disappointment, or a complaint. By then, the relationship may be compromised. Proactive care, in contrast, builds a strong foundation for the inevitable challenges of life. Having empathy enables professionals to relate to others in the myriad aspects of ever more complicated lives. These deeper relationships involve taking a personal interest in others' families, hobbies, charities, and preferences. Achieving success on these fronts prepares one, with a ready-to-listen ear, to know, like, and trust their advisor. The challenge is that we let few people besides close friends and family into the inner circle at critical moments of life such as marriage, birth, and death. Occasionally, we allow a lawyer, money manager, or member of the clergy into the circle yet we shy away from our financial advisors when we need them most. Why?

So much has been written on the hard, analytical left-brain side of financial advising: how to create a financial plan, manage a portfolio, account for insurance needs, etc. Fewer resources explore the soft, nurturing right-brain aspects of such relationships. Tim Owings masterfully bridges the gap. An excellent whole-brain advisor, Tim is perhaps uniquely qualified to address all aspects of the client relationship, given his training and practice as a pastor, financial advisor, and teacher. In fact, Tim's unique gifts and interests qualify him to circumvent the hard aspects of financial planning with a sincere care and love for his clients, who are indeed blessed to have him. What one quality determines the future of the strongest and most complete advisor-client relationships? It is the ability of advisors to master both sides of this sometimes arduous connection. As Tim asks, "Will advisors listen with ear and heart?"

I first got to know Tim when he sent me two high-quality, emotionally compelling CDs of Christmas songs with him at the piano. They were amazing! I could tell from our brief back and forth via email that he was a person of substance. And I consider it a privilege that he asked me to write this Foreword. As you will discover, Tim Owings is first and foremost a caring, curious, observant and respectful human being, with special talent and interest in communicating how to care for clients meaningfully and intentionally. As Tim puts it, "It's that other half of the work—the half that is more demanding but infinitely more fulfilling and satisfying—that will separate you from all other advisors."

Allow me to preview some of my favorite lines in the book, without comment:

> "Language moves between the left and right brain. In the financial services business, the temptation is to use the left cerebral hemisphere exclusively—rational and numbers oriented—because that is what we put on paper.

> "Continually add to your advisory catalog textured right-brained pictures that place the client's story in the middle of the scene. See yourself as an artist who specializes in the intermingling of this inventive neural network. You will discover powerful tools to connect with clients that become bonds no hiccup in the market will break.

> "George Bernard Shaw noted, 'the single biggest problem in communication is the illusion that it has taken place.

> "I have noticed that clients breathe a lot easier when we grant them permission to place a comma in the decision-making process.

> "Not every call, email, letter, or meeting need be about business.

> "Meeting with nervous clients on their turf makes them more comfortable.

> "[In times of difficulty for the client,] be fully present and offer hope.

> "My assumption is that all of us step into the advisory business because we want to assist others in bettering their lives. It is a ministry of sorts whereby we create a satisfying and rewarding career for ourselves."

As you might see, Tim Owings is indeed a different type of financial advisor, and more importantly, an exceptional man. His appeal for a holistic approach to practice management transcends the basics of creating and implementing a financial plan. Tim advocates becoming a major player in the orchestra of your clients' lives.

He suggests (correctly) that it is equally important to know and care for all human beings during their victories as well as their personal, family and career defeats. Put your clients' needs first and watch things fall into place naturally. As you implement the concepts in this book, decisions become easier, relationships thrive, people like and trust you more, and referrals flow freely. When care is front and center in your practice, clients will take care of you through their loyalty and appreciation. Getting this right is not always easy and doesn't come overnight, but it has the power to transform your practice and perhaps your life, too. I encourage you to read on.

Bob Doll
Nuveen Asset Management

17517-INV-O-07/17

Preface

An unexpected event happened in my well-planned life more than a dozen years ago. The profession for which I had trained and in which I had worked for over 25 years came to an abrupt halt. I will get to that part of the story in the pages that follow, but for now, we go to the beginning of this odyssey in 1975.

Barely out of college and newly married, Kathie and I packed what few belongings we owned and moved from the familiar rhythm of south Florida to Louisville, Kentucky—1,000 miles from family and friends— where I enrolled in seminary. Eight years later, with Master of Divinity and Doctor of Philosophy degrees and three children holding three of our four hands, we moved: first to North Carolina, then Alabama, and lastly, Augusta, Georgia.

Thirteen years into my ministry in Georgia, I made a tough decision. The church I served was plagued with leadership issues I was unable to mend. On my 50th birthday, after months of an agonizing soul-search, I resigned. The church graciously provided a generous severance that allowed me the precious gift of time. In those first weeks and months, I reflected on my ministry and invested time to reconnect with family and contemplate my future.

Six months later, in late 2003, I gained employment as a stewardship consultant with a national church fundraising firm. Every week for three years, I flew coast-to-coast, helping churches and non-profits raise capital to expand ministries and retire debt. Changes within the company, as well as the physical drain of traveling cross-country with extended stays in barren hotel rooms finally took its toll. The story then took a surprising turn. A week before Christmas 2006, Kathie and I reconnected with a couple we had known for some time. Our reunion took place at a piano concert I give each year for the Augusta community. The following day, the husband emailed a note to wish us a Merry Christmas, expressing how pleasant it was to see Kathie and me. I glanced down the screen and "Financial Advisor" stared me in the face. "That's right," I thought. "He works with a large investment firm." I responded and asked if I could take him to lunch before the New Year. He immediately wrote back and suggested his manager join us.

Two months later, I went to work as a financial advisor-in-training. The next eight weeks, I studied feverishly: first for the Series 7 and later the Series 66 exams. I passed and secured the insurance licenses needed to begin my new career. In late June, after two weeks at our firm's national training center, I went into production and began building my business.

I was fortunate to have rewarding friendships and acquaintances that enabled me to grow a list of prospects who before long became clients. Two veteran associates in our branch became my mentors. After three years of successful solo practice the three of us formed a partnership, combining our books of business.

I relied on my pastoral skills to enhance the planning and investment strategies I was implementing for clients. One encounter after another confirmed these honed shepherding skills was one of the reasons I was having such success. I learned what every capable advisor knows: clients only work with someone they trust, respect, and believe is competent. I learned one thing more: taking the time to incorporate traits such as empathy, sincerity, patience, and sensitivity fosters a connection with clients. So, how might others draw from my experience? Could I teach advisors how to integrate into practice the core competencies clergy use in their work? Imagining such an approach found me envisioning an advisor-client experience restructured and redefined.

Cadence of Care: Imagining a Transformed Advisor-Client Experience is a reflective journey that joins the personal and pastoral skills I honed in the ministry with the work of an advisor. Merging these two seemingly unrelated skill sets has been deeply rewarding. Ministers, by virtue of their training and work, know how folks are wired. What if advisors offered professional, competent counsel infused with imagination and an extraordinary level of care?

What you hold in your hand is not a book about sales. However, deeply caring for your clients will generate and grow more sales. This is not a book about client service, but being with clients when life caves in on them will forever redefine your definition of service. Conversely, this is not a book outlining a system of management; nevertheless, advisors who learn to attune their instincts to a client's varying emotions will ultimately manage their practice better.

This is a book calling advisors to a greater discernment of the issues clients often endure alone. What follows is not so much an arsenal of silver bullets or a tool box of quick fixes. In many ways, you will be looking at yourself in the mirror of your own life story. My hope is you will begin to use these insights in your professional and personal affairs. Whether it is listening or presence, explaining investment options or pitching your tent in your client's story, this approach will become a trusted partner in everything you do. While most of the principles I espouse are characteristic of my pastoral and current advisory efforts, they easily translate to the professions of accounting, banking, law, medicine, teaching, and other care-centric occupations.

The one question for me that will not go away is, why write this book? As I gaze at row upon row of excellent volumes written by talented financial gurus, who am I to throw my two cents into the advisory conversation? In order to answer that question, let me briefly take you back more than 40 years to a defining time in my life as a 19-year-old college student.

In the early 1970s, my generation was experimenting with competing lifestyles. Rock and roll had morphed into heavy metal and many moved to the beat of Janis Joplin, Cat Stevens, The Rolling Stones, and Led Zeppelin. Some of my friends were dangerously using illegal, even lethal psychedelic drugs such as LSD, heroin, and speed. Others had escaped from the confining cage of parental expectations; instead, they hit the road to explore America! Hair was long and beards were full. Muslin tunics, wide collars, and bell-bottomed pants were avant-garde. An unpopular war raged in Southeast Asia. Society's tempest waged war against oppression and cultural biases. Many of my peers served in Vietnam. Some did not come back. Though many Vietnam vets returned to productive, meaningful lives, a few touched down on U.S. soil emotionally broken and confused.

Richard Nixon resigned the presidency. The U.S. economy began a ten-year period of market stagnation and unprecedented inflation. Those were the years when the once gleaming vestment of imagined post-war solidarity tarnished. In the previous decade, a President's assassination and civil rights leaders' murders left many questioning whether the Cleavers were analogous to American family life.

During those tumultuous years, unprecedented numbers of my generation entered seminaries and prepared for ordained ministry. Most chose that way for very good reasons. All did so with the belief a life of service was the needed salve to heal our fragmented and hurting society. In 1972, I too felt a calling—a divine nudge to train for and become an ordained Christian minister. Long hair, bell-bottoms, and wide leather belts notwithstanding, I wanted to make a difference in the lives of others. Therefore, I said "Yes!" to a life of ministry.

Through training and experience, clergy learn there are numerous entry points to connect with parishioners. Preaching a sermon, teaching a small group study, visiting the sick and shut-ins, talking with an elderly congregant confined to a nursing facility, tenderly holding the hands of the dying, and celebrating with newlyweds and new parents are some of the duties that punctuate the career of an effectual ministry. This calling, rife with idealism and naiveté, is the fuel powering a seminarian's course of study and a new minister's first assignment. Such was my path.

In time, idealism's bloom withered under the brutal heat of parish reality. Over the years, a harsh truth moved into my well-designed, idealistic home and established a noisy, disruptive presence. It happened so slowly I failed to recognize that, at least for me, congregational politics had become poisonous. I found it impossible to be active on a board or participate in a civic activity without it sapping what little energy I had left after holding the hands of the dying and poring over a fresh sermon week after week. There were always budgets to manage, personnel policies to administer, money to raise. With a staff to lead, endless committee meetings, competing egos, and conflicting agendas, not to mention a wife and three children who needed me more than I realized, I eventually came to the end of my personal and spiritual resources. I never doubted God's presence in my life. My work, especially the warm relationships I enjoyed with parishioners, was deeply fulfilling.

In time, I came to question my ability to function at the highest level my role required. The calling to be a compassionate leader evaporated under an institutional hot sun. Unaware of my own vulnerability, I professionally burned out. I had pastored five churches: from a rural village chapel to a 4,000-member megachurch where I was responsible for 50 employees, a popular televised outreach and a budget in the millions. After 25 years I said, "Enough!"

My family and I have volumes of warm memories from those five congregations. We experienced a level of respect and affection few ever know. The congregations we served loved us and in turn, we loved them. But by the time I walked away, I was so far removed from those early, passion-induced, idealistic dreams that I had almost forgotten what they were.

The life-story that has brought you to choose an advisory career may have vague similarities to mine. You too may have stepped away from another profession where energy and optimism simply died. Perhaps it was a calling that no longer felt right. Cynicism, regret, or disenchantment may have taken you down unimaginable roads. My assumption is that all of us step into the advisory business because we want to assist others in bettering their lives. It is a ministry of sorts whereby we create a satisfying and rewarding career for ourselves. As my first manager taught me, "You never really help another person without also helping yourself."

Despite the rewards, soon—and in the financial services business, very soon—your practice obligations take precedence. Developing your approach to the work, onboarding assets to manage, growing your client base while remaining current with industry regulations and market perspectives take time. Early idealism gets lost in the balancing act of building a profitable business while meeting the expectations of clients. You might ask, "Is there enough of me to go around?"

Each of our stories is unique to the life we have lived. That said, I assert that every advisor, regardless of his or her history, wants to serve caringly those who look for direction beyond a monthly statement or annual review.[1] A voice within us whispers unceasingly an invitation to ask of our clients the more profound questions and to listen attentively for the answers. Repeatedly, we are offered an opportunity to peek through the dark veil of a painfully worded sentence, while intuiting our clients' need for the warm and caring touch of someone who really hears them.

So here I am, in this good work of being a financial advisor. With more than nine years in the business, and drawing on nearly 30 years of pastoral work interwoven into the multi-colored tapestry of my life, I present to you an uncommon approach to client care. I am convinced every advisory practice can experience renewal by incorporating into daily routines the ideas prescribed in this book.

As you read the following pages, you will see how the content and exercises presented in each chapter gradually become the rules rather than the exceptions. As you hone your craft, you will develop a system by which to include these useful tools in every client encounter. Doing so creates "Aha" moments as you realize why they are so vital to your success. Recall defining moments that created the person you are today. Jot down memories in the margins of your mind. You will see—perhaps for the first time—the trajectory your life has taken. Allow your story to resonate throughout the halls of your life and practice. You may find yourself on the road Robert Frost so memorably described as, "the one less traveled." It might make all the difference.

To make that distinction, begin by reimagining your practice and reflecting on the twists and turns of your life and those of your clients. Chapter 1 challenges you to define important moments in your clients' lives, from their earliest years. You will learn how attitudes radically shape their understanding of money, wealth, and risk. When you know and value each, the path clears for you to move to a place of empowerment as your practice begins to transform.

In Chapter 2 and throughout this book, we examine what causes us to use language poorly or inaccurately. George Bernard Shaw noted, "The single biggest problem in communication is the illusion that it has taken place." We will explore our use of language to avoid falling prey to such an illusion. Clients need not have majored in English to question what we said and what they think they heard. Keeping that in mind, we will look at frequently used phrases that send the wrong messages. Additionally, how might word pictures bring clarity to a discussion? Together we learn how the surprising language of music and "conversational punctuation" create places for reflection and awe.

Chapter 3 explores the powerful dynamic of active, reflective, imaginative listening. In the course of our waking hours and, perhaps during deep sleep, we hear audible and intuited sounds: judgments, cars honking, birds singing, feet shuffling, phones ringing, even our own heart beating. Familiar voices of broad-casters, a colleague, a client, a loved one, all make their way into our subconscious. This chapter illustrates how we can better interpret a client's unspoken messages.

Listening then merges with the vital, dynamic discipline of learning. Chapter 4 will dare you to become a life-long student of yourself and your clients. This self-assessment is an advisory core competency. From our early years and beyond, we associate learning with the structures of a classroom, a college or university setting, a continuing education seminar, a trade book, or the rigor of pursuing the CFP® or CIMA designation. But learning—constant learning—is making mental notes on what you observe every step of the way. The best lessons are experiential; they come from others' actions or inactions, thoughts and attitudes, prejudices and biases, as their perspectives mirror our own at that precarious intersection on the journey of discovery.

The next two chapters unpack the broad subject of emotions; how they shape our personal stories together with those of our clients. Chapter 5 examines the poisonous nature of anger and how it negatively impacts every aspect of life through its venomous bite. In contrast, anger can be the impetus to rouse other passions, inciting positive action. Chapter 6 looks at dispositions that eke their way into the advisor-client relationship: happiness, sadness, disillusionment and more. In all candor, if we could take emotion out of our money decisions, we would be better served. However, removing emotion from other decisions would be detrimental to our lives. And still, feelings capture the better part of our earthly experience. They course through our veins, supplying us with a vital force that sets us apart from all of God's other creatures.

Chapter 7 offers techniques for "Advising Through Loss," exploring its pervasive effect on our states of mind, and how advisors can equip themselves to offer support when grief shows up. So many of us believe death is life's ultimate loss, but some would confess that a life unlived is the greatest loss of all. Sometimes we are besieged with unexpected sorrow. We may have early memories of losing a family pet or a favorite toy. As we age, we will undoubtedly experience the demise of someone or something special to us. A wholehearted approach to care is required if we are to overcome the pain of loss.

Chapter 8 looks at basic people skills, how we engage our clients and how they perceive and accept us as trusted advisors. Undivided attention to one's countenance, attitudes, availability, and overall nurturing presence may determine how successful we are. Do we have the conviction that our work will revolutionize clients' lives? Are we confident in our approach to financial management? Are the talents we bring to clients first vetted in our own experiences? Is compassion integrated into who we are and the way we relate to others?

These questions force us to look at an opposite but equally important factor. Chapter 9 exposes limitations in our work. The boundaries established by the license(s) we hold, the policies of the firm for which we work, and the compliance labyrinth we navigate every day all place restrictions on us. Clients and advisors alike operate within their respective confines. No one is omnicompetent.

Chapter 10 reexamines our need for regular communication. Not every call, email, letter, or meeting need be about business. In fact, the more we touch base with clients concerning the mundane, the stronger will be our connection. Checking in is the outward expression of nurturing presence as we weave deliberate, non-business interactions into our routines. Clients stay with advisors who return phone calls, text messages, and emails in a timely manner. And yes, they welcome other sides of our personalities when we call to discuss current and local happenings. The closing chapter asks five critical questions calling us to lead with purpose. A review of the topics and actionable ideas will demonstrate how care leads to stronger, more rewarding connections and collaborations.

You may discover, as I have, that this work becomes a creative, celebratory art form. I encourage you to get to know your clients' hopes and dreams. Investing more time in them supports their need to clear imaginative space where they again believe in themselves. Doing so, you will detect anew the pulse in your practice steadily beating. This care-centric approach requires you to conceptualize your business as an impassioned calling and to see the work you do in an inspired light.

This is an open invitation to integrate selflessness, compassion, and care with the needs of your clients. So keep reading. Ask penetrating questions about your own journey. Recall failures and successes. Relish the joy you found on the other side of pain. Be grateful for the person you have become.

Next, go to www.timowings.com, bookmark it, become a subscriber and create a dialog between your colleagues and the book in your hand. Then, imagine arriving at the end of your career. What do you want your clients to remember about you? What will they say when they think of the times you simplified a planning issue or showed them returns on their investments? It is nice to hear, "He knew me and my family." "She was there when I lost my parents and danced with my son at his wedding." "He was the best listener." "She cared deeply for my family and me and all of us knew it." And yes, "My advisor is such a trusted friend." That is what I want my clients to say about me.

Those precious client memories are priceless. They reflect the cadence of care, the depth, and sincerity of your interactions and become the legacy you leave when you clean out your desk and turn off the lights. Let us now see where this journey takes us as together we learn simple steps that help us become the supportive, caring advisor we all want to be and in so doing, transform the work we do, the people we serve, and ultimately, ourselves.

Tim Owings
Augusta, Georgia
July 2016

Chapter 1

The Stories We Find Ourselves In

We are born into a drama that has played on history's stage a long time. We learn from our earliest years that we are all actors in an expansive cosmic enactment, participating, but not as its star. Eons before our parents conceived us, perhaps even long before we were an imaginative twinkle in their eyes, the plot of this miraculous narrative was unfolding to include us.

When we showed up in the story, the continents and oceans had been teeming with life for millions of years. Though we arrived late, our presence now informs and often controls how everything exists on planet earth. Humanity now takes center stage. We are born to play our part as characters in this drama. Advisors play a singular role as our narratives intersect with another's story. These intersections between advisor and client are constantly forming. To appreciate this powerful reality, to invest in learning our personal history and the narratives of those we serve is to modify every factor of our business. The challenge, of course, is making that investment.

So how do stories inform our work? In broad strokes, as we converse, problem solve, plan, and manage assets, our lives converge. The temptation—often unconsciously—is for the advisor to focus only on the business at hand. If we stop there, we miss vital information that contributes to a client's life from infancy to the present.

In their excellent book, *Storyselling for Financial Advisors: How Top Producers Sell,* Scott West and Mitch Anthony unpack the importance of learning the client's story as a vital tool in the sales process.[2] The thought-provoking questions they recommend we ask are powerful. Our narrative, however, is equally important.

We may think we know our story well yet remain blissfully ignorant of how moments in our childhood onward have shaped who we are. We live comfortably within a cocoon of morals, perspectives, and beliefs bequeathed to us by family, some healthy and others potentially toxic. Together they create the person we are and mold who we become. The same is true with our clients. What has happened to them at a particular time, whether note-worthy or routine, radically shape who they are and what they understand. At times, their story is so dominating, they cannot hear what you, the advisor, are saying.

My life bears witness of this sensitivity to the past. At 13 months of age, less than two years before the Salk vaccine was widely available, polio showed up and forever changed me. My parents, devout and faithful, found themselves asking if God had cursed them. Seeing polio's devastating impact on my body—a withered left leg and an obvious limp—softened their resolve to adopt a new mindset. Mom and dad never told me I was physi-cally challenged; instead, they gave me piano lessons. They knew I would confront my own limitations, so they stoked the fire of music. After years of lessons, recitals, and public performances, music remains for me a burning passion. Polio's unpleasant reality did not cripple my spirit. In fact, it contributed to the positive, resilient, and strong-minded person I have become. I have a limp, but the limp does not have me! If I were your client, would knowing how this childhood affliction shaped my attitudes help you understand me better?

In every facet of our work, the advisor-client story runs on parallel tracks and merges in interesting ways. As we dive deeper into our clients' lives and learn about their upbringing, we come to understand how one's parents felt about money and success, adversities and triumphs. This preponderance may color invest-ment recommendations or moderate a portfolio's risk tolerance. On the advisor side, getting in touch with our own issues regarding money, investing, and financial responsibility clarifies how we hear and interpret what our clients are telling us. Though this work takes a personal commitment of time and resourcefulness, knowing and valuing our stories empower us to do our best work.

THE ADVISOR STORY

The caring advisor chooses to invest time, energy, and reflec-tion in coming to terms with her personal story. I think every advisory training program should dedicate an entire day to focus on self-awareness. Everyone in class would be asked to write a two-page autobiography focused on people and experiences that have shaped their formative years.

- *Parents*

Who were my parents? What memories do I have of my ancestors? Were there ethnic or language dissimilarities that set them apart from the communities in which they lived? What do I remember about their siblings? How would I describe the way they were reared: poor, affluent, middle-class, educated, religious, political, divorced, widowed?

- *Education*

What memories do I have of my early education? What value did my parents place on reading, math, science, the arts, and sports? Was being educated understood as something you accomplished or, was it a lifestyle of learning?

- *Conflict Resolution*

How was conflict resolved? Do I have memories of domestic violence? Did I learn how to fight fair when observing my mother and father having a difference of opinion?

- *Money*

What role did money play? How did my parents manage money? Were they employed or did they own their own business? If employed, was the company small or large? Local or national? What did I learn from them about money, investing, and fiscal accountability?

- *Loss*

When tragedy, loss, or death befell us, how did we handle our grief? What role did religion, spirituality or faith communities play in our family? How do I now handle loss in light of what I learned?

These types of questions serve as the background for writing one's personal story. The narrative does not have to be long, but it must be reflective, critical, and above all, honest. An advisor who grew up in a lower-income family where manual labor put groceries on the table will have a different money perspective than an advisor whose memories are of country clubs, golf lessons, and exotic family vacations. This is not a judgment call, but rather an observation noting the divergent histories of the men and women in advisory professions. In my office, I work side by side with colleagues who have disparate family histories, yet all are doing excellent work.

Acknowledge your personal script. Take a sobering look at your history and identify areas in your background that reveal clues into your personality. Remaining out-of-touch with the good and bad of your past will handicap in some way your ability to move into the client's world with integrity and candor.

Parental Investments

Reflecting on our lives while asking the introspective questions listed above, we find out that each of our parents deposited gifts in us from their personalities, perspectives, fears, and faith. These gifts, or investments, create a psychic dividend stream that pays out its wealth throughout our days.

One of those parental investments is what the Germans call *Weltanschauung* or worldview. Parents shape the matrix by which we see our lives. Was life welcoming or threatening? Was the world a buried treasure or was it a deserted island of unseen dangers? How were outsiders viewed? Did they merit confidence? This parental perspective tempers how we interact with others.

The second investment parents make in us is a passel of emotional-spiritual resources. How did you observe your parents relating to each other? Was your mother a strong and independent woman or was she subservient to your father? Do you have memories of seeing your father and mother cry and grieve in the face of loss, sickness and death? How did your parents handle anger, frustrations, or disappointments?

Our profession touches on many stark realities. When advisors look into the catacomb of histories bequeathed them by parents, revelations come to light. Perhaps my concern over a client's handling of a six-month bear market is me remembering again my father's anger when he lost money on a failed joint venture. Could it be that my inability to be more empathetic is rooted in my parents' handling of grief and loss? The emotional and spiritual investments families make in our formative years stay with us and shape how we respond to various situations.

The third but surely not the last investment parents make in us is attitude. In our formative years, was the proverbial glass half-full or half-empty? Were conversations around the dinner table

lively and hopeful about the future or did we receive a heavy dose
of "the world is going to hell-in-a-handbasket" negativism? Viktor
Frankl, the celebrated psychiatrist who survived the horrors of the
holocaust wrote, "Everything can be taken from a man but one
thing: the last of the human freedoms—to choose one's attitude in
any given set of circumstances, to choose one's own way."[3] Frankl's
timeless words demand we ask ourselves: "How do I manage my
outlook? Do I embrace the gift of life that greets me with the rising
sun or do I pull the cover over my head and begrudge the day?"

Advisors who dial into the power of attitude have an incredibly nimble resource to help clients face the fluctuating realities
with which they contend in every season. It is my conviction that
advisors reared in a negative, pessimistic environment can choose
to move the needle of their emotional compass toward hope and
optimism. That needle may not move quickly, but move it must
if your vision is to help men and women reach goals in spite of
obstacles. Parental investments leave, in some way, their mark on
our lives. Ignoring how these investments shape one's life robs the
advisor of valuable resources to pull from and use during client
interactions.

I vividly remember sitting in a dear friend's office listening
to him talk about his family. Though we had known each other
for more than 15 years, windows flew open on this octogenari-
an's fascinating life. His eyes sparkled with love as he talked about
his dad.

"I grew up in a coal mining community in southwestern
Virginia where my father was the company doctor. He saw everybody from infants to seniors. I have fond memories from my
boyhood of going with my dad to a home in the middle of the
night where he delivered a baby."

When he told me his father began his medical career on
horseback, I listened with even greater attention. I sensed a
convergence of our lives. Over the course of an hour, Bob, who
within the next two months became a client, shared fond recol-
lections of growing up in a coal mining community as an only

child. Known throughout town as the son of Dr. Moore, nothing of privilege or entitlement found its way to him. He learned the benefits of hard work, earning and investing money, and that no matter what, there would be no whining, complaining, or excuses for not becoming his best self. In a later visit, I sat with his wife Maryann and listened as she shared her memories: how the two met in college and the joys of their incredible marriage, early years together, and starting a family. I saw parental imprints that swayed their outlook on the world that, decades later, was still shaping who they were becoming.

It was that early visit in the first months of building my practice that a searchlight cast its beam across my life. As they discussed their lives, I remembered my father's work ethic and principles—even his personality. Like Bob's father, my dad was fiercely independent, a "type A" personality who allowed no excuse to get in the way of accomplishing any goal. During that first visit, I exclaimed, "How I wish our dads could have known each other because the man you describe is so much like my father." Over the years, I developed an attentiveness managing their portfolios and being fully present to them. I am grateful for the relationship I have with Bob and Maryann.

Echoing off the walls of everyone with whom we work are the voices and values of immediate family members, contributing an inimitable perspective on who we are and what matters most. Those parental investments take up residence and refuse to relocate. Advisors who get in touch with their story, starting with their family of origin, bring to their business a focus that cannot be quantified. That said, another power imprints itself, prompting our immediate attention.

The Historic Matrix

An advisor growing up in the 1970s will have an understanding of life dissimilar to one who grew up during the 1940s. When we thoughtfully write our narrative, we perhaps see ourselves as a

10-year-old, within a family, community, and the world. We ask, "What was I observing and feeling at that time?" For me, growing up in Miami, Florida left me with vivid memories of the late 1950s and 1960s. I recall a close-knit community shifting from English-speaking to one that was mostly Hispanic. Though my world was evolving, my reality stayed much the same. I continued to ride my bicycle miles from home without thinking about this mutable landscape, never once concerned for my physical safety. Such were the days of my childhood.

This was not so for children who grew up in the '80s and '90s in large American cities. Gone were the days when most children walked or pedaled their bicycles to school. Parents had a much higher concern for their children's welfare; a concern that reached new highs. In the 1950s and 60s, there was no such thing as the Internet or cellular phones. We stayed in touch with friends and family via a clunky rotary phone and watched G-rated programs like "I Love Lucy" broadcast from a 19" black and white Sylvania television set. That is not the case today and has not been for over 30 years.

Whereas I grew up during the Cuban missile crisis, crouching precariously under desks during bomb drills, children today arrive at school greeted by security guards and metal detectors. They see adult content on the Internet and the threats of terrorism and death loom over their lives daily. The context in which you were reared leaves sociological and political properties in your spirit that cannot be washed off with soap and the running water of time.

As you reflect, ask yourself questions such as: What did my old neighborhood look and feel like? When I was 10, who do I remember as President and what did my parents think of him? Was the topic of politics openly discussed in our home and if so, how often and with what degree of emotion? Did my mother or father serve in the military? If so, how did their enlistment shape my opinion of the world? Is history moving toward a more civilized or a more brutal future?

Like the gift of *Weltanschauung*, each person's historic matrix shapes how he or she sees the succession of time. While parents subtly impose their understanding of the world on us unawares, others stroll through the turnstile of our lives affecting how we interpret reality. Do you see how this cognizance might color client engagements? In significant ways, an advisor sees the world as the thoroughfare on which a practice travels. Place history in the context of generation and geography. Those variances contribute to who you are.

Significant Others

Parents shape our stories and influence whom we attract into our lives. People with whom we are closest often mimic the perspectives we received from our family history by adding their unmistakable flavors to the mix. If married or in a committed partnership, one's intimate companion contributes to how we structure and commune with the world.

My wife and I have been together for many years. Though I continue to bring to our marriage the beliefs in which I matured, her influence on me is great. She has taught me, through observation and instruction, how essential it is to validate someone's feelings. Her keen discernment of underlying emotions is nothing short of remarkable. I have watched her absorb a friend with a level of understanding that makes me take note of her kindness. I am the student; I sit straight, listen, and learn. That said, however, she too is bringing to our marriage the distinctive behaviors of her parents. The same is true for work associates, neighbors, and acquaintances with whom I share a mutual bond.

The men and women with whom I have had professional ties for over 40 years have added rich and lasting gifts to my life. Naming those gifts and placing great worth on them brings a strength to my work which would be lost if I failed to be mindful of them. If you, like me, reflect upon the valuable deposits given you by significant others over the years, you uncover a wealth of treasures. Most of those treasures add incalculably to the relationships you work so hard to establish and maintain.

So where does this take us? At the least, remember the names of those who contributed to your story, capturing those generous gifts. Advisors who plow through the daily grind of working with clients and staying current with professional requirements while ignoring their story are advisors blindly walking down a road where the bridge is out. Why? Because overlooking the manifold contours of one's personal life robs the advisor of perspectives as intimately individual as one's fingerprints. Elevate your profession from simply doling out advice to becoming cognizant of the wealth of experiences you bring to those you serve. Open that treasure chest of your story, discovering its wonder. Now follow me as we learn the client story and see how it informs our own.

THE CLIENT STORY

The exercise of putting together our own story using the questions in the previous section now comes to bear on the story of every client. True, we are not psychotherapists and cannot make such a claim, but we can, particularly when we are at a dead end, fall back on what we have learned about our clients' stories. I point you to the Appendix, an advisor-client conversation guide. There, you will find a variety of questions and topics that serve as a roadmap for client discovery. A downloadable version is available at www.timowings.com.

Let us fast forward in the process as if you are now familiar with events that influenced your client's life. How do you responsibly use the information you have gleaned? Is it appropriate to say back to your client what you heard him say about his parents, where he was reared, and how others may have contributed to his perspective? Absolutely! However, the necessity of repeating what you have heard must be done with sensitivity and compassion. So how is this accomplished?

Perhaps the best way to answer that is for you to eavesdrop on a composite of two or three conversations I have had with clients. The names, identities, and circumstances were changed to protect confidentiality.[4] This discussion emphasizes knowing your story and the client's story when making critical decisions. Imagine having this talk and note how your background might create the context to hear what I heard.

An Advisor-Client Conversation

The setting for the appointment with Allison is my office on a crisp Wednesday afternoon in autumn. I move from behind my desk and sit beside her where there is no physical barrier between us. Client visits work better for me when I have a relaxed seating arrangement.

For several years, I have been an advisor to Allison and Rick. They recently divorced after 24 years of marriage. Rick had entered a substance abuse treatment program late in their marriage and his inability to maintain steady employment was contributing factors to the couple's parting. I was able to keep both as clients, working with their attorneys and the court orders that have retitled their assets with the firm. The relationships built and nurtured with Allison and Rick have engendered their faith in my ability to help them during this unpleasant time. They have been open with me about their lives, allowing me to offer a higher level of professional support. I transitioned beyond the expected planning and financial management of their accounts to become a trusted advocate.

Tim: Allison, it's good to see you this afternoon. How has your day been?

Allison: It's good to be with you Tim, especially after the recent days I've had at work. As you know, this time of year we are inundated with cases all wanting some resolution before the end of December. The days have been long, not to mention I'm taking a lot of work home.

Tim: I understand your stress, but your voice is telling me it's especially rough right now.

Allison: (Looking away from me for a moment, she then turns and looks back.) Thanks for understanding. And you're right. Not only am I feeling the weight of parenting, but the work staring me in the face is overwhelming.

Tim: (With an understanding nod, I shift a bit in the chair so I can make better eye contact.) Are you saying you don't have time to unwind, recharge your batteries, and grab dinner with a friend?

Allison: That's it exactly. What I wouldn't do to have an evening with my college roommate Cheryl. She probably thinks I've dropped off the face of the planet. I mean, we swap Facebook photos of our kids and update each other on what's going on, but that's not the same as being with someone who really understands me and has known me since we were freshmen at Rutgers.

Tim: Allison, if memory serves, you shared with me some years back the story of how your dad started his business when you were seven. Doing the math, that would have been around 1974. Am I remembering that correctly?

Allison: Exactly! In fact, I have memories of seeing my dad very little during those years—really between my 7th and 13th years. He was constantly at work. Up early, home late, building a tool and dye business that started in an abandoned garage. Over time, he grew it to annual revenue in the 20-million-dollar range.

Tim: Your dad and your mom really embodied the American dream of building a business from nothing to a thriving, successful enterprise. That's something to be proud of. And yet, I know you needed your dad but he was unable to be there for you.

Allison: You have a good memory. Yes, I can still hear my dad starting his car before dawn, as I got ready for school. And night after night, I watched him eat his dinner around the same time I got ready for bed. He was incredibly successful, but oh, how I wanted time with him in those early years.

Tim: (As I listened to Allison share this memory, I noticed her eyes moisten). I wonder, Allison, if this drive inside you to work day and night isn't somehow linked to a message your dad and mom sent you during your childhood—and perhaps even later?

Allison: What do you mean? I think I have an idea, but you go ahead.

Tim: As you know, I'm not a psychotherapist, but I do know from having taken a focused assessment of my life that some of the messages given me by my parents cannot be turned off. Much like your parents, I grew up in a blue-collar family and neighborhood, the child of a World War II veteran. My father and mother wanted my siblings and me to live better than they had. Neither were college graduates, but they were certain of the importance of education.

Allison: That's the message my folks gave me. In fact, my dad's business success and the support my mother gave him in that venture, even though she held down a part-time job as a legal secretary, made it possible for me to attend a school like Rutgers and then on to Harvard for my law degree. My parents were amazing!

Tim: They were, indeed. All of us have a story that walks through our lives every day. We carry with us messages about work, education, faith, society, injustice, wealth—you name it! These messages are relentless. I wonder ... is there a way to schedule down time with Cheryl and get back to the gym two or three days a week? Sometimes, we must turn off the work message and turn on the self-care message.

Allison: (Before responding, she again looks off as if she is gazing at someone's face beyond the 6th-floor window of my office.) The work isn't going away. I know it won't be easy, but I can do it. I deserve it, my children deserve it, and my clients deserve it. You said what I needed to hear in a way I wouldn't have heard it had you not taken me back to those early years. I am so grateful for the good gifts my mom and dad gave me, but I have to offer myself one now.

Tim: And Allison, the gifts you give yourself will afford you the opportunity to be a more resourceful attorney and supportive mom. (I paused and took note that Allison was embracing more of her own story, seeing the value in making time to address her needs. She then looked at me.)

Allison: Tim, you always know how to listen to me. You compel me to see what's most important. (She shifts slightly in the chair as she reaches into her purse, pulling out an index card.) Now, I guess you're wondering why I asked you for some time today?

Tim: It has crossed my mind, but we needed to talk first about you, didn't we?

Allison: We did, but here's what I need to discuss. We need to talk about Lisa's study abroad expenses for the spring semester and Kyle's scholarship applications to State and Wake Forest.

For the next 20 minutes, Allison and I worked on her business issues. We said our good-byes after visiting with each other for more than an hour. The following day, I sent Allison an email summarizing our conversation and the financial matters concerning her children. I ended the communication with a parting sentence assuring her of my support as she makes more time for herself. Two days later, I dropped her another email saying, "I'm cheering you on! Let me know if there's anything I can do for you in the weeks ahead."

Taking the time to learn Allison's story years prior was a critical factor in my ability to listen to her. Knowing her history, along with my own, gave me resources to be there as a supportive friend and advisor. Investing in a client's story is something I routinely do to get to know them and for them to become acquainted with me. While listening to Allison, I recalled my life as a teenager in the 1970s and remembered how I felt about our society. Our lives collided during that hour and brought to mind memories of my own that spoke to the stresses she faced.

When we place ourselves in our clients' situations, we create a bond of trust and an environment of acceptance. No clever strategy—no matter the financial reward—will replace the investment an advisor makes in knowing well his own story and taking the time and energy to learn every client's story. Stories matter. Narratives are the steel girders below the surface that help us withstand the ebb and flow of the markets and the economic tempests blowing through our lives.

In the following chapters, we explore how communication, emotions, and personal limitations add color to the interpersonal plot that is continually unfolding. Staying mindful of these dynamic forces may take our practices to unimaginable places. I offer you an uncommon perspective on how to engage others and how advisors can become even more impactful to those they serve.

LOOKING BACK

■ Coming to terms with our story supports us in our work as advisors. The efficacy of parents, the historic era in which we were reared, and the significance of others have shaped who we are and how we see ourselves.

■ Everyone is living in a drama that has been unfolding from birth. Investing the time to learn a client's pivotal life moments provides a greater understanding of how advisors ultimately work within the relationship.

■ Knowing the extent of client assets, the dreams they have for their future, and dialing into the power of story all enhance client engagements and endow advisors with a higher level of competency.

NOW WHAT?

1. When you think of your parents, what words or phrases come to mind that positively shaped who you are as an adult?

My parents were part of "the greatest generation." They were thrifty, hardworking entrepreneurs. Deeply spiritual, they incessantly gave their best gifts to all. My dad's creative imagination was held in check by my mother's practical wisdom. Together, for more than 60 years, they reared four children, all of whom have college degrees, successful careers, and loving families.

2. Reflect on your parents' character, financial acuity, work ethic, and friendships.

From age six, music has played its role and added its power across every page of my history. My parents at times sent confusing messages about what held our family together. In retrospect, we had no more or no fewer challenges than all families face. I remember three major job changes in my dad's life and my mother's return to work when my older two siblings went to college. Money was tight, but I never experienced fear or lack of security.

3. Bring to mind the names of clients whose histories you know well. Have these stories affected how you understand who they are and what is relevant to them?

Clients' stories intersect in our minds. We see patterns in attitudes towards risk, concerns for retirement and/or future health-related expenses. When you work with a new client, imagine one or two of your existing clients sitting with you. What have their stories taught you that advance the work you are doing?

4. What is the one thing you plan to share with clients going forward that will help them better understand who you are and how you see the work you do?

We control what of our past we want our clients to know. Identifying three or four turning points in your life and being able to express those "Aha!" experiences will provide handles for your clients to hold as they work with you on planning and investment issues.

Chapter 2

Language:
Lost and Found

All living organisms on planet earth use language in some way. Whether it is simple DNA coding at the cellular level, the grunting of gorillas in the Congo, or creatures who own multiple delivery systems, all living things communicate. Anthropologists tell us that early on, *Homo sapiens* devised systems whereby thought became sound, and sound words, and words structure, and structure language. Long before the rise of Sumerian cuneiform or Egyptian hieroglyphs, humankind conveyed to one another information, emotion, and stories about themselves and their mysterious world. Ancient texts like the Gilgamesh Epic, Homer's Iliad and Odyssey, the Hebrew and Christian testaments, the Hindu Bhagavad-Gita, and scores of other narratives give evidence to the power of language in the service of the story.[5]

Advisors traffic in information, concepts, images, numbers, and reassurance. How we use language reveals more about who we are than one can possibly imagine. When we pen a sentence or speak aloud, our personality paints itself on a page or tumbles out of our mouths belying who we are, what matters to us, and the level of importance we place on speech. George Bernard Shaw immortalized this phenomenon in his play "Pygmalion" that later came to Broadway as the musical "My Fair Lady." Henry Higgins, a linguist of some renown, makes a bet with Colonel Pickering that he can transform a typical cockney flower girl into a sophisticated lady whom he will pass off as royalty to London's elite. Higgins, who knows English like Mozart knows music, has the frightening ability to ascertain the exact place of one's birth simply by listening to a person speak. Bernard Shaw's Higgins was more the student of language than any of us will ever be. If you are familiar with the musical, you know his character was brilliant but not very sensitive. Unlike Higgins, might language well used in all its forms be a way of expressing care?

Mark Twain said it best: "The difference between the right word and the almost-right word is the difference between lightning and a lightning bug." Let us take a quick excursion through the fascinating and empowering language landscape. Like a gifted painter, we create landscapes of ideas on the imagination's canvas. In a like manner, music has its own syntax. The minute we infuse rhythm into a conversation, vibration becomes sound, sound becomes voice and voice meaning. When the advisor employs language well, clients hear and understand at an emotive, action-focused level.

First, I offer a confession. I struggled with English throughout my elementary and high school years. In fact, I retook college freshman English three times before I passed with a C—gratefully! It was not until I signed up to take a Greek language class as a college junior that the English grammar and usage lights turned on. Learning Greek under the thoughtful tutelage of Dr. Naaman Keathley forced me to learn my own language. How did that happen? One of my Greek homework assignments required that I take an English sentence and translate it into Greek. That exercise forced me to recognize grammatical constructs, and subsequently an appreciation of my own language while learning another. Two semesters of Greek improved my ability to write and speak English, leading in part to my completing a Ph.D. in New Testament Literature and Greek.

Moving forward, I emphasize where we may be speaking poorly as well as affirming where we are using language properly. Compliance will flag us on objectionable words and phrases used in client communications. My list of what to avoid and/or erase from our vocabulary is equally valid, yet often ignored. The goal, however, is to foster a heightened commitment to deliver an advanced degree of care. If you have not heard your own voice on a telephone call or taped and listened (with permission) to a client meeting, you are missing an unsurpassed learning experience. So let us travel on this "lost and found" highway and see how we might use the alphabet, images, phrases, even music as tools to respect and care for our clients.

YOU MEAN WHAT?

Some 40 years ago, deeply immersed in learning the language in which the Christian New Testament was written, I had a conversation with a gifted Greek scholar who became my professor and dear friend. The late Frank Stagg was Professor of New Testament at the seminary I attended. One day I needed to purchase a Greek lexicon. As we chatted in his office, Dr. Stagg offered me sage wisdom. "Dictionaries," he said, "do not so much define words as they reflect usage. That's why publishers reprint them year after year." One of the reasons the multi-volume *Oxford Dictionary of the English Language* [OED] is such a useful tool is because it defines and *shows* a word's usage in literature.

Languages are continuously adapting to the times, and not always for the best. What is *cool* may have nothing to do with temperature any more than what is *bad* may actually be "cool." What follows are a few terms that have wormed their way into our vocabulary. As you read, make a mental note of other idioms that simply say the wrong thing even as they reveal a speaker's attempt to say the right thing.

The first we must rethink is the response *No problem*. The contemporary use of this phrase unwittingly conveys a negative message. The subtle implication is I could have been a problem! In my world, I hear this response on the telephone four, five or more times a day. I will often ask, "Could I have been a problem?"

"What do you mean?"

"Saying 'No problem' implies I could have been a problem or, in the past, I've been a problem. Am I?"

There is silence until the other says, "Oh my. I had no idea I came across like that!" It might be inconsiderate of us to suggest to a client how to speak, but when a client thanks you, have your positive response be "You're welcome" or the Ritz Carlton's "My pleasure." When we go the extra mile, when we listen supportively to client stories and support them through a painful time, we say from the heart, "It's an honor and a pleasure to serve you." A conscientious advisor pays attention to and places a high value on using words accurately.

In our desire to be transparent and clear, other phrases that have crept into our vocabulary are, *to be honest*, and *truthfully*. We will often begin a sentence with "To be honest" suggesting we *could* be honest, perhaps less than honest, or—horror of horrors—even dishonest! "Truthfully" is equally toxic. My gut tells me advisors may lose business because of shooting themselves in the foot with these misleading terms. Instead, ask, "May I be candid?", "To be frank," or "Candidly." Advisors who build their franchise on ethics and deep discovery must be, by definition, transparently honest. Anything less than that maligns our calling, diminishes our stature, and may even destroy our credibility and reputation.

The verbs *need*, *ought*, and *should* cry out for review. Having delivered more than 5,000 sermons during my active pastoral years, I know how clergy unconsciously traffic in these three words. Moreover, there are times when we absolutely *need* to change the way we look at language; when circumstances dictate an *ought* or a *should*. Instead of saying, "I think you need to raise the level of your insurance coverage," say "It's important for you to consider increasing your insurance coverage." In the first sentence, the advisor is insinuating a need. The second sentence seizes on the power of what is crucial.

An equally impactful way to avoid the use of *need*, *should* and *ought* is to assertively state, "It would be prudent of you to have an

appointment with an attorney to go over your estate documents"
rather than say, "You ought to see an attorney and update your
will." In each instance, you exude self-confidence while making
your client feel they are making a wise choice. None of us enjoys
hearing what we *ought* to do. Yes, it requires sensitivity to your
own voice, even to the point of being self-critical. Not only will
you, the speaker, move from language weakness to strength, but
you, the advisor, will provide a measure of care that honors those
with whom you speak.

My list of misnomers now hits home. I question *No way!*
You're kidding! and *Wow!* every time they leave my mouth. I must
find other words that are less dismissive. I want my response to
sparkle with amazement and wonder! "You're kidding"—in client
conversation—may diminish another person's sincerity when, in
fact, there is nothing flippant about what they have said. More
appropriate might be: "Impressive!" or "I see why this got your
attention." These found words are better suited, softening an
otherwise carelessly used expression.

The language of our senses is a powerful tool to evoke a respect
for the hearer that is immediate. Pygmalion's creator, George
Bernard Shaw, spoke volumes about the incongruent use of the
English language when he said, "England and America are two
countries divided by the same language." We may divide our clients
from ourselves using conventional slang to convey unintended
messages. On the other hand, we transcend accepted customs and
bridge an uncomfortable divide with positive, affirming figures of
speech.

The goal in client engagement is respect for the other person's
concerns. Using language thoughtfully becomes a gift that has
clients saying to themselves, "My advisor is a professional whose
keen mind and warm heart personify the type of person I want
around me." Language may not be the most powerful weapon in
our arsenal, but it is the one we most use. For that reason alone,
we must use it well.

WORD PICTURES

Don Connelly is, in my judgment, the best in the business when it comes to teaching advisors how to connect with clients using imaginative analogies and simple stories. If you have not heard or been the beneficiary of Don's work, go to www.donconnelly.com and sit at his feet to learn how to paint pictures in clients' minds. I take Don's work on the sales front as a jumping off place to apply his word picture principles to client care and support. The following examples use the colors, plot, and emotion we glean from client stories, plants them in the advisor's imagination, and feeds them back to the client in vivid, remembered images. Weave them into conversations and watch them quickly connect the dots of the discussion.

The first word picture that comes to mind right out of this fast-paced existence many of us live is the freeway. My client Richard's story included professional advancement opportunities and career interludes. During a meeting, I said, "Rick, as you've traveled the career freeway these past 20 years, I've noticed times when you took an exit ramp that connected you to the next opportunity and how that took you and your career to higher ground."

"Yeah, most of those off-ramps took me to places I couldn't have imagined except the time I foolishly turned down a dead end!"

"It didn't take you long to get back on the right road. Now, my friend, I'm seeing you running low on fuel, physically worn out by a job that has rewarded you handsomely, but I'm not sure you know where you go from here."

Richard dropped his head a bit and nodded in agreement. "I love my work," he muttered, "but it's about to get the best of me."

"I wonder if you could see a rest stop up the road another mile or two?"

"What do you mean?" he asked.

"You're in need of a professional 'Rest Stop.' Get off the highway and stretch your legs. With the energy you bring to everything you do, you must take better care of yourself."

We talked substantively about his taking time off to rethink where he now was and to map out where he might go in the future. The highway image was an apt depiction for this highly driven man.

Word pictures take up the craft of storytelling. They rest the mind's rational left brain, while inviting the imagination of the right side to paint a landscape captured in technicolor. Books, television, the theater and film flow in and out of our lives on multiple levels. Each offers an explicit view into ourselves, others, and the future with an unsuspecting twist. Using word pictures such as the metaphor of the freeway with exits and rest stops transports clients to a place where the mind sees the self in a dynamic way.

What about a sparkling diamond? A small number of flawless diamonds exist in the world, commanding prices only the ultra-wealthy can consider. Gemologists use a grading system to establish the four factors of classification: clarity, color, cut, and carat weight. These factors describe the matchless qualities of a diamond. Few are rare. The majority are beautifully blemished gems that have minute inclusions only seen with a monocular and other examining instruments. The same is true of our multi-faceted lives. Often scrutinized and inspected by the world at large, our defects appear bigger than they deserve. We allow circumstance and discord to cloud the beautiful jewel that we are. Numerous flaws come from our genetic code. Siblings are born tall and short, blond and brunette, with blue eyes and brown, each exhibiting delightfully unique personalities. Some of us gray early; others appear ageless. We are all jewels with beautiful flaws! When clients invite advisors into the inner sanctum of their lives, they allow us to hold up to love's light their hopes, dreams, and fears.

A third word picture that connects client stories to the care we offer is the garden. Though I am not a gardener at present, I take you back to the time I served a rural congregation in southern Kentucky. There, in that bucolic, postcard-like village, Kathie and I planted our first garden. We grew Irish potatoes, broccoli, beans, tomatoes, onions, squash, corn, and cucumbers. We were "city slickers" who knew nothing about farming. Our parishioners made bets among themselves as to what would come out of our half-acre plot. To all of our amazement, we grew bushels of vegetables. We canned, froze, and pickled our harvest. The large yield of Irish potatoes we kept in our cool basement.

What if we imagined every client's life as a cultivated garden, where edible plants, fruit trees, and wildflowers add beauty and nourishment? Such a garden requires a lot of work, patience, and no small degree of luck. The rains have to come at the right time, pests of all sorts will do their best to harm or destroy the crops, and weeds seem forever out of control.

Suppose you asked a client, "What if you imagined your life as a garden? In the back are rows of corn beginning to tassel. To the left are beans maturing that need to be picked. The cucumbers out front are growing so fast you have to pick them every other day. Looks good, doesn't it?"

The client nods and says, "Where are you going with this?"

"Let's look at something else growing there and I'll answer your question."

"What's that?"

"In the back-right border of the garden are fruit trees and a 50-year-old walnut tree. Near the left-front, I see rows of colorful zinnias, daisies, and lilies that you cut every few days for your kitchen table." The client looks puzzled, but you go on. "What if your life is more like this garden, teeming with fruit and nut trees, vegetables and flowers? Decades ago, someone planted that walnut tree. Year after year, you collect, store, and share the nuts with friends and family. Six years ago, you planted the apple and pear trees—call them investments in the market, your children, a career, friendships—that are now yielding fruit you will enjoy for years to come. The flowers are the bond you have with your mate, the beauty in your painting, music, golf game, hunting, or another hobby. And the vegetables are the product of a career that literally puts groceries on the table and allows your family to enjoy a prosperous existence."

This one-word picture awakens our imagination, but the power of the image is clear. Anytime we take a client to a relaxed place is time well spent. Why? Because all of us are better when we allow ourselves to step away from those things that need our attention. A client does not have to have a green thumb for you to take them to a garden and show them how their work, their days, their energies are creating bountiful crops. Who would reject an invitation to sit for a few minutes in a cool place made beautiful by lush trees, blooming flowers, or a babbling brook singing in our ears? When clients decide to see the beauty of life in another way, they walk away better.

Golf legend Sam Snead provides us a fourth word picture. Years ago, Snead took up the problem every golfer has gripping the club. To address that problem, he likened the grip of the golf club to the way one might hold a bird with two hands. You must, said Snead, hold the bird in your hands tight enough so it does not fly away, but not so tightly, you kill it! This image perfectly instructs a client with teenagers how best to guide those young lives toward adulthood. Teenagers need parents to hold them securely enough so they do not fly away unprepared for the independence of adulthood, but not so tightly they rebel and reject wisdom and discipline.

Advisors hold clients in their hands much the same way; we show up in times of misfortune and loss, inviting them to share and voice their concerns. Clients count on us to help them reach their goals and dreams. We must be careful not to grip them so loosely as to shank or drive them in the wrong direction. Then again, if we hold clients too tightly, they lose a sense of autonomy and empowerment.

These four images are not even the tip of the iceberg when it comes to illustrating concepts. Learn what brings joy to your clients—whether sports, music, travel or hobbies—and use those favorite pastimes to help them see something they would have missed without your assistance.

Language moves between the left and right brain. In the financial services business, the temptation is to use exclusively the left cerebral hemisphere—rational and numbers oriented—because that is what we put on paper. Continually add to your advisory catalog textured right-brained pictures that place the client's story in the middle of the scene. See yourself as an artist who specializes in the intermingling of this inventive neural network. You will discover powerful tools to connect with clients that become bonds no hiccup in the market will break.

THE LANGUAGE OF MUSIC

As a musician, I am passionate about the language of music. During music's romantic period (1780-1910), composers like Franz Liszt, Richard Strauss, and others created tone poems; symphonic works that evoked vivid images rooted in that era's perceived reality. These works captured a time of sweeping political, religious, and economic change in Europe. In contemporary society, an advisor does not have to be a musician to appreciate the power of music. In every age, music enlivens the spirit and is a commentary on the times. If your client is younger, you might use a line from a current hip-hop, country or pop song to illustrate an idea. Older clients might relate better to music from the 1960s or '70s or a classical masterpiece. Music, with its sound and lyrics, connects people to more memories than any other artistic gift. When I hear a Simon and Garfunkel song, I am immediately back in high school. There I am, driving my 1960 Corvair (a rambling wreck) to Miami Springs High School for my 7:00 a.m. class, with the warm Miami breeze buffeting my face, and the 8-Track tape player pumping out "The Sound of Silence." It only takes a few chords of that song and all those memories dance to the beat in my mind, taking me to a special place in my past.

Ask your clients about the music they most remember from their teenage years, what they enjoy hearing now, and the artists with whom they most connect. Some clients know the lyrics to country songs better than they know their blood type. Other clients are aficionados of the classics and are invigorated listening to a Mozart piano concerto or the operas of Verdi. That said, how do you paint a picture with a sound, a tune, a lyric, or a timeless work from the classics? It is really quite simple. As you get to know your clients, you may hear them tell you about an instrument they play or favorite songs they enjoy. A client who loves rock and roll may have recently attended a concert in your city. Ask her, "Did you happen to go to the Bruce Springsteen concert a couple of weeks ago?"

Over time, we learn where clients may fall on the music spectrum. In conversation, connect the love of music to your clients. For example, the client who likes the saxophone will understand when you say, "John, this idea we're talking about is like jazz. In the moment and improvisational, it takes a melody and plays it four, five, or six ways. In a trio, the piano, bass, and drummer each takes his turn interpreting the line, the beat, or both. Right now, you are going through an improvisation. You are taking the big song of your life and reimagining it. Big corporations call it innovation. In essence, you are creating a new genre of music."

The opera constructs another realm of word pictures. I understand opera is the most expensive art form because it requires a large hall, an orchestra, elaborate costuming and staging, and (highly paid) singers to bring the story to life. A client who has gone through a painful financial or relational loss may see that experience as a tragic scene from her life's opera. In Verdi's "Rigoletto," the lead realizes his daughter Gilda is involved with the villainous Duke of Mantua in a way that ultimately leads to her death. There, on stage with the orchestra intoning somber lines, Rigoletto's impish character transforms itself into a grief-stricken father as he discovers his plan has gone bad. He has paid an assassin to kill the Duke; a deal with the devil that has instead led to the death of his beloved daughter. Our plans, no matter how well intended, turn in unforeseen directions, often because of something we did or failed to do.

Music is a language all its own. Imagine a movie without a soundtrack, a commercial void of its jingle or even a Jeopardy game without that haunting theme song dancing through your mind as the clock winds down and contestants write the final question. Picture a restaurant with its soft music streaming continuously throughout the day. Music plays a major role in our lives. With constructive use, it becomes a means to enrich our business.

CONVERSATIONAL PUNCTUATION

The third part of language lost and found is how familiar punctuation marks define the spoken language we use. Punctuation is a necessary ingredient of syntax, or the way words and phrases design a sentence. Have you thought much about how you construct a conversation? In what follows, I explore how punctuation marks facilitate the verbal back-and-forth between personalities. This is a novel idea, but follow me and let us see what we might learn.

The Period

The most misused conversational punctuation mark is the period. Some advisors rush through meetings too quickly. When they do, clients may feel pressure to make a decision about something not fully understood or, if they do understand, do not like. A period says conversation over, work done, and for us, next appointment. Most clients may dislike this abrupt finish while never letting us know it. When a client believes an end is imminent, she may believe that in the advisor's mind, whatever was being discussed is now resolved. The client, however, has not reached the same conclusion.

So when do we punctuate a conversation with a period? Obviously, there are episodes that end: the placing of an insurance policy, an annuity, or sadly, a death. Clients who update their estate documents rarely want to extend that work over weeks or months. When a client is considering life insurance, there is only so much time after the underwriters have made an offer in which a determination to secure the policy can be made. Otherwise, as you know, the application reverts to underwriting and the process starts all over again. Once finalized, the task is completed.

The majority of decisions we advise clients to make, and those they know they must make, do not move quickly to conclusion. Planning resolutions require the period, following a time of gestation in the client's mind. Mulling over the sale of a business involves multiple layers of due diligence. Accountants will tell you that choices about depreciation, asset acquisition, property management, and redeployment of capital have T-I-M-E written all over them. In most cases, avoid this rush to the period in favor of a pause.

The Comma

More and more, I end client conversations by saying, "Let's put a comma here and take this up the next time we visit with each other." Even the shape of the comma—that descending, slightly curved line—suggests a pause, even a break in the real or imaginary sentence. Commas invite room for questions, fears, and ideas not yet discussed. Advisors who learn the power of the comma and master its use give to clients a higher level of care and the rejuvenating power of patience.

I have noticed that clients breathe a bit easier when we grant them permission to place a comma in the decision-making process. You will see it in their faces, hear it in their response, and welcome the time to turn over in their minds what we see clearly but for them remains out of focus. Commas say to the client we respect her time and need to work through whatever stares her in the face. What we perceive as procrastination is her need for additional time and carries far more weight than our need to close a sale. Clients warm to the pause and will take us up on unfinished business after a week or two when we artfully use it to their advantage.

Insert a comma in conversations and enjoy your clients' reaction to sensing it there.

The Question Mark

A conversation's question mark fuels the curiosity gene in every advisor-client encounter. I am not talking about asking questions, although doing so is Rule One in developing client rapport. This unspoken interest may be nothing more than a slightly raised eyebrow that asks, "May I know more about that?" An advisor with an inquisitive mind connected to a caring and compassionate heart is a professional who will always have clients.

When we walked through the stories we found ourselves in, we learned the importance of asking questions. Those narratives revealed the way our lives have unfolded. Now we must inquire into every aspect of a prospect's life as we guide them through the process of becoming a client. Open-ended queries invite another person to tell her story in her own way. The temptation lurking beyond the Q & A session is to assume we have all the information we need and that the person responding has shared with us exactly what we need to know.

Now go into a larger area furnished with more of the questions clients have of us than we may have of them. This room is loaded with uncertainties that, left unaddressed, cripple our ability to help our clients, even those we think we know well. Clients may toss us a question mark when we divulge something about our own investing history, fears, and mistakes. The question may be left unvoiced, but you will hear it if you watch your client's reaction.

The Colon and Semicolon

The colon and semicolon in a conversation serve as a merge, the unscripted space where a sentence and the other person's verbal or non-verbal reaction meet-up. The colon, as we know from 10th grade English, is the punctuation mark that precedes a list. "Thomas picked up a number of items from the grocery store: a head of lettuce, three potatoes, fresh broccoli, a loaf of bread, whole bean coffee, a two-pound roast, and a ten-pack of paper towels." The semicolon, on the other hand, completes an initial thought and begins an extension or further explanation of what came before. "Alice spent the morning choosing jurors for her defense of a product liability case; a trial that had so much publicity she was only able to approve three jurors, rejecting ten for conflicts of interest." These familiar punctuations typically mark a division in a sentence. They function the same way in a conversation. They create a transition in which we ask the "Are you confused?" question or say, "Let me offer you a story." How a client hears us has much to do with the perspective he has on a particular subject or an emotional issue blocking his ability to figure things out. Take the time to introduce these breaks into your conversations and you will develop a better way of communicating.

When you sit with clients and they with you, remember this language back and forth is always taking place, whether spoken or unspoken. We listen and revisit what comes out of our clients' mouths within the framework of what we have already learned about them. We who traffic in advice have so much to say worthy of a listening ear. Unwittingly, we can bulldoze right over these subtly sent conversational punctuation marks, missing the opportunity for a verbal rest, a pause, a uniting of minds and emotions—a moment signaling our need to be clearer. This slowing down allows us to hear what could be a vital message the client most needs us to hear.

The Exclamation Point

The exclamation point is language's applause, what for us is a silent "You did it!" "I'm so proud of you!" These are messages clients crave. From the moment in infancy when we first focused on another face, we found energy in reading that wider smile, a twinkle in the eye, and "I'm so smitten with you" message. I have seen it in my own children's faces as have you. That moment when they have done something so enthusiastically, so meaningful to them, they look at us for the thumbs-up that says, "You're amazing!"

Clients need that reaction from us when they stay invested through a correction in the markets or grasp a planning proposal that will benefit their family's future. Conversational exclamation points are spontaneous smiles. When a client unexpectedly shows you more of himself than even he meant to disclose, react with an exclamation point. These moments surprise us. When we walk a client through an idea that uses a word picture and they get it, the stars align and all is right in the world. We wrongly disassociate spontaneity with professionalism. Such a disconnect not only weakens the ties that bind us but robs us of sharing those joyous expressions of delight that turn an ordinary day into something of wonder and satisfaction.

Develop an affinity for these five conversational punctuation marks. Feel the pulse of a conversation as your clients offer you an unrestricted glimpse into their lives. Ignore them, and you miss untold opportunities to capture nuances that define who they are and what matters most to them.

LOOKING BACK

■   Language travels down the highway where feelings and thoughts become words, images, and ideas, revealing our commitment and need for vital connections.

■   Without self-awareness, we revert to using words and phrases inaccurately and at times, insensitively.

■   Dare to paint pictures that "show" more than "tell."

■   Just as we punctuate the written word, learn to punctuate conversations and notice how clients hear you with accuracy and greater interest.

NOW WHAT?

1. When was the last time you listened to your own voice? Professional and amateur musicians record their music to refine their

craft. Subtle adjustments to a violinist's bowing technique or a singer's vocal resonance dramatically affect how we hear that artist. Ask clients if you may record your conversation and tell them the reason: "I'm focused on speaking concisely and want to hear not so much what you say, but what I'm saying and how I say it." I have presented this to my clients and they gladly agree. It is as if I hear them say, "Tim wants to be better at what he does."

2. Add a word picture to your vocabulary every week. Make it a game. As you read the newspaper, listen to a reporter or anchor on television, notice how media professionals creatively use them. Clients must see, feel and at times touch a concept before fully understanding it. I have used a small bowl of paperclips to describe a mutual fund, with each clip representing a stock or bond. I dump the clips out on the desk and explain, "A mutual fund manager selects investments to put in the fund he or she manages. Some funds have 30-50 stocks or bonds, others over a hundred." As I talk, I put the paperclips back in the bowl, one at a time, to demonstrate my point.

3. Infuse every conversation with punctuation marks. Like you, my schedule gets very crowded; the time during client visits often flies by. Remember that clients notice our seeming to be in a rush or our lack of interest. Punctuation marks create energy and place crucial spaces in a sometimes hurried exchange of words.

Chapter 3

Focused Listening

As I reflect on my life, I recall men and women who became confidants for many reasons, not the least of which was their caring heart and listening ear. No matter the circumstances, people who hear and understand us forge a bond that rarely breaks. We know from experience that active, focused listening requires energy. When others believe we are hearing them, they tell us more about who they are and what matters most to them. Advisors unintentionally create more problems than solutions when they fail to listen reflectively, critically, and carefully. Listening's gift measures its beat in every phase of our work.

One such moment occurred the day my client Mary and I were meeting for a semi-annual review about her investments. For nearly 30 minutes of asking me to repeat myself, and seeming lost elsewhere in thought, she failed to mention her father's declining health. I knew for 6 months that her dad had suffered a stroke and, after 10 days in the hospital, had gone to a local nursing facility. Still mentally sharp, but physically weakened, her dad's main concern was for the welfare of his wife, my client's mother, a breast cancer survivor now on the downside of remission.

When she said for the third time, "that depends on how my parents are doing," I intuitively jumped off the meeting's agenda and said, "Mary, let's stop for a moment. It seems you are especially troubled about something going on with your mom and dad." As if a spigot had turned on, Mary shared with me weeks of stress over her mother's deteriorating health and the lack of care her dad was receiving in the nursing facility. If that were not enough, her 23-year-old son had been arrested for DUI and was facing jail time and the loss of a semester's work at the university.

The more I listened to Mary's story, the more her portfolio evaluation settled unnoticed into a dusty corner of my office. She was so overwhelmed with the issues in her parents' and child's lives she could not consider anything I said related to her accounts. After listening to her unwind what seemed like endless reels of sadness, she looked at me and said, "I know you weren't expecting me to dump all this on you, but I so needed to get that out of my soul. Thank you for being here for me."

The task at hand is not the contracts, signatures, the audit, or the deal. Yes, clients hire us to address and manage financial and business issues but often, they cannot focus, bogged down by other demands. What they need from us during those times is a willingness to listen with a sensitive ear. Advisors must take the time and the emotional risk to do listening's hard work, remembering how deeply we feel valued when someone invests the time to listen to us.

For over 20 years, a pastor in the city where I live has, without fail, been there for me through thick and thin. He is a friend, mentor, and exceptionally perceptive listener. His face shows concern, his eyes radiate love, and his responses unfailingly express compassion and understanding. When we are together over coffee or a meal, he invites me to say whatever I need to say. I have thought much about why my friend is such a good listener, arriving at the same answer every time. He is comfortable in his skin and knows himself well. He silences the other voices for an hour, creating an uninterrupted space to hear me.

I realized that for most of us, the highest hurdle in listening is muting inner voices. Being innately egocentric, we must allow ourselves permission to invest the time, energy and focus on something or someone other than ourselves. To pay close attention to the person speaking to us is to tap the priceless treasure that falls in our lap when we practice focused listening. More times than not, we misunderstand more than we understand. Our ears hear what is coming out of another's mouth, but we often come to inaccurate conclusions. We think we know the client's perspective without asking for clarification. We quickly put together a response before we have the whole picture in focus. Hearing a string of words, be it in the context of a business conversation or over a cup of coffee with a friend does not equal comprehension. How we put together what we thought we heard can be daunting.

Like you, I have read many books and heard numerous talks about active listening. That simple skill follows this process:

1. Listen to what the other person is saying.
2. Repeat back to them what you heard for accuracy or correction using the phrase, "I think I heard you say _____."
3. Listen for validation of what you believe you heard.
4. Confirm messages by saying in your own words what the other person said or what you think they meant to say.

Still, if active listening is so simple, why are we continuously failing at the task? The answer may come from an unexpected place. Actor Alan Rickman, who died in January 2016, was perhaps best known in his later years for playing Professor Severus Snape in the Harry Potter movies. During a broadcast on NPR in the fall of 2013, Rickman reflected on his stellar career in the theater and film. A handful of sentences from that interview may advance the art of listening.

"I think," said Rickman, "that being lucky enough to have worked in film, with hindsight, actually helps you in the theater because it encourages you to know that to watch somebody thinking is interesting and also to watch somebody listening is interesting. So I think that's been quite a profound influence to me on stage as an actor and as a director."

Now lean in. "And, I would say, that if I have learned anything that boils down to one phrase it would be that acting is about accurate listening."[6]

Whereas active listening attempts to understand the message, focused listening goes a step further. As Rickman rightly noted, focused listening involves two people hearing each other while simultaneously watching the thinking and listening of the other as each bridge the communication chasm. Focused listening infers that when we are with clients we are on stage enthralled in an art form. If "acting is about accurate listening"—and I allege Rickman expressed what I have known for years—then as clients watch us listen to their words and thoughts, we rehearse this art form as if we are performing on the stage of the Globe Theater in London.

Watching a client think, speak, and listen calls for a penetrating degree of attention like no other. Such cognizance receives far more than words exiting a mouth. Simple, often ignored details such as posture, a nod, and other gestures are key indicators in conversation. For our part, we must scan the mind's hard drive and extract previous conversations with that client. What was unsaid, misheard, or overlooked months or years ago? What might we have uncovered had we been more attentive and read between the lines?

BARRIERS TO EFFECTIVE LISTENING

Interpersonal interactions can be thorny even under the best of circumstances. My wife and I have been married more than 40 years. We still have moments when we misread one another's motives, emotions, and bearing. There are times when we simply cannot hear what the other is saying because of the distractions of the day. For advisors, barriers to effective listening might be a glaring television, emails and appointments popping up on a computer screen, a notification sounding on a smartphone. Addressing these is easy: turn off your devices. Drive out the interruptions and be still if but for a moment, receiving the message and the other's need to be heard.

Other Voices

Musicians who play one of the instruments that comprise a traditional band or orchestra learn early on that their part is one of several in the ensemble. Full orchestras include four sections: strings, woodwinds, brass, and percussion. Look at the graphic on the following page. What you see is a wondrous moment in the Rachmaninoff Piano Concerto No. 2 in C Minor from the conductor's score of the Concerto's first movement. The various instrumental parts are all there, starting with the flutes at the top straight down to the strings at the bottom. The piano (P-No) part, two-thirds down, has the soloist playing one of many magnificent passages in this work. I show this to you not because I assume readers are musicians, but to illustrate what is going on in all lives from one moment to the next. When we sit with another, whether in an advisory capacity or casually with a spouse, child, or friend, multiple instruments are playing on both sides of the conversation at the same time.

We may only hear the delicate sound of the flutes, a dramatic melody from the strings, or the impassioned playing of the piano. The instruments, heard or not, are all there playing together. To acknowledge the presence of these colliding messages is admittedly problematic. Our personal agendas contain volumes of information and feelings that are always firing across the scores of our minds. At any given moment, a client may be reminded of an errand she has to run during her lunch hour. Distracted, she hears in her mind the voice of a spouse talking about a date with friends on Friday. On the advisor side, there is a client visit across town scheduled in two hours that will require timing the drive just right, going to a dental appointment early the next morning, and preparing and filing a tax return. The adage "if it's not one thing it's another" rings true for both.

As we learned in Chapter 1, advisors who recognize life's intricacies are more responsive when clients share their history. Understanding messages from our past, both good and bad,

Rachmaninoff Piano Concerto No. 2 in C Minor
First Movement

allows us to rid the mind's landscape of pervasive rubbish. Such a clearing forms a space to hear the other person because we have purposefully made our own story a partner. These speaker-hearer connections, watching and listening to one another, connects dots in both parties' minds that clear a path for greater clarity and understanding.

Stories in Conflict

For me, growing up in south Florida during the 1960s and '70s colors any conversation I have with a person whose background includes ethnic diversity and societal transition. In the same way, having lived with a physical impairment, I hear a client talk about a special needs child in a way others may miss. This personal identification with another creates a warm and inviting atmosphere where we connect at deeper levels.

Sometimes, however, our stories incite potential conflict. For instance, we may hear a new episode in a client's story that dredges up a prejudice long dormant in our minds. Some years ago, I was visiting with a friend whose story I thought I knew. We had known each other for more than ten years, shared church and community ties, mutual friends, and enjoyed many of the same pastimes. One day over lunch, he mentioned that his brother, married and a father of two, had told the family he was gay. As I listened, I heard a judgmental inner voice saying, "Glad that's not going on in my family," and "How could such a thing happen?" The more my friend talked, the less I could hear him because this inner, conflicting and negative voice would not shut up!

I failed my friend that day. Only after the passage of time did I come to the place of even recognizing what had happened during that revelatory conversation. What he needed from me was someone who indeed felt his pain. What he got was a person he assumed he knew well who was, in that moment, hypercritical and incapable of offering support. Months later, we saw each other at a community gathering and found a private place to talk. I asked how he was handling his feelings and how the family was navigating this new reality. After a few minutes, I said to him, "I owe you an apology." Taken aback, he asked, "Why?" I communicated my failure to be a trusted friend and asked him to forgive me. Our time together opened new avenues for us to connect with each other, thoroughfares we travel now with greater discernment.

When we give and receive messages, two or more lives collide. More often than not, contradictions surface and vie for attention. When a discordant voice sounds off in your head, be intentional and turn it off. Advisors who listen for conflict have a great opportunity to make it an ally by finding neutral ground. When you and your client part, entertain that voice, accept its perspective, or toss it.

The Absence of Tools

Have you noticed in private and public conversations how some believe that saying something louder makes it more true? In those moments when I am not sure or want to make a point, even at the expense of the facts, I will raise my voice and say whatever I feel compelled to say. The third barrier to focused listening sits in this shared space. Clients look to us for information, solutions, and support. Advisors see themselves as sources of these core competencies. When we do not have the answer to a problem, we may keep talking even though we know we are unsure of what we are talking about. Let us call it the terror of doubt. When fear shows up, we may raise our voice, offering less than accurate information.

The absence of tools contaminates our ability to be focused listeners. The client has asked us about the tax implications of an investment or an estate planning method we vaguely remember from our training. Those kinds of specific questions may run headlong into our internal voice as it attempts to find some response hiding in a cobwebbed corner of our memory, tuning out the client speaking to us. We not only miss what the client is saying, but this terror of the unknown quickly hijacks our better judgment.

When a client or colleague asks me a question that immediately raises this fear, I say, "I'm not sure of the best way to address that concern," or "I have to look at that issue and get back to you." In other ways, when lack of knowledge or uncertainty rears its head in a conversation, quickly address that voice freeing you to listen to all that follows. I have never had a client reveal a lack of confidence in me when I have said, "Let me get back to you on that issue." Clients warm to advisors who admit they have a knowledge gap while expressing a commitment to fill it.

PARTNERS IN FOCUSED LISTENING

Focused listening must be a collaborative experience. By that I mean we engage in conversation with others aware of trusted partners who enhance and validate what we hear another say. These partners are not other people, but rather allies in the quest to hear and understand. Using the imagination, we bring these partners into every conversation. Emily Dickinson beautifully noted, "the possible's slow fuse is lit by the imagination." In what follows, and in every conversation, light this slow fuse of imagination and see these trusted partners sitting with you as you visit with and listen to clients. In the room with you are four empty chairs on which these partners sit and hear what you hear. Wise is the advisor who learns the relational power of these partners who will become trusted friends. Study the diagram below. The four imaginary partners hear and see everything with you. How does this work?

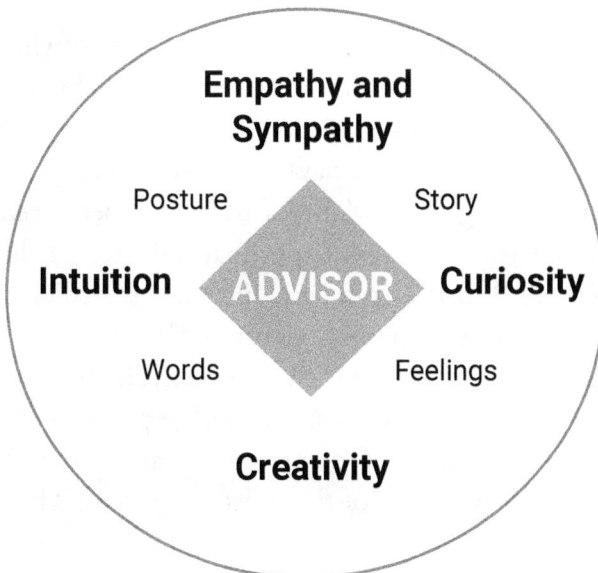

Empathy and Sympathy

Empathy and its cousin sympathy are the first partners in the work of focused listening. Two sides of the same coin, they convey to clients an unparalleled depth of care. Both feelings deserve a closer look. Let us first consider empathy. Derived from the Greek word *empatheia*, the word is a cognate of the Greek preposition *em* meaning "in" or "with" and *pathos*, from which we get the word passion. Expressing empathy suggests we suffer with another because we have experienced something similar in our lives.

In contrast, sympathy, from the Greek *sympatheia*, puts *sym* "together" with *patheia*, "suffering," meaning to suffer together or to suffer alongside another. We offer sympathy when our life experience differs from another. You are *with* them, but have not experienced the brutal suffering through which they now journey. Anyone can employ sympathy. Preface an expression of concern by saying, "I've not been where you are or experienced the pain you are now enduring, but I will be here for you." That is expressing sympathy with integrity.

Conversely, there are times when we can say with integrity, "I know exactly how that feels because, like you, I lost my mother after a long battle with Alzheimer's." That ability to suffer with another's situation, having been there yourself, is at the core of empathy. When you work closely with people, you will witness all manner of human discord in their lives. Years on life's timecard give us the right to employ empathy. We have been to the cemetery to bury loved ones. Some have watched helplessly a child go down an unforgiving road. Many of us have experienced illness and its aftereffects. We have known financial stress, failure, and recovery. We have learned from pain, but these tragedies need not always leave us feeling helpless or victimized.

Age, life experience, failure and restoration, illness and recovery authorize us to hear our client's stories and respond to them with understanding. The gifts of compassion, care, sympathy, and empathy are at the very top of those listening tools. They enable us to do excellent work with and for those they serve. Take a few minutes and look at your own life. Take notes from the uneven roads down which you have traveled. Pause. Ponder those times when your life came to a complete halt because health failed, a relationship ended, a close friend received a tough diagnosis or a work situation went awry. How did those complete stops alter or redirect your perspective on the meaning of life and who and what matters most to you?

With time and practice, focused listening becomes integral to our advisory work. As we invest the emotional collateral of our lives, we are then able to apply what we have learned as our clients share their stories. Listening does not happen in a vacuum. It is dynamic: two speakers, two listeners, two life stories swap words back and forth. This active conversational matrix, to be effective, must engage empathy and sympathy if only because you have chosen to be in touch with your own "stuff." Such self-awareness creates an empowering space to be with your clients when those very difficult seasons of their lives show up.

Curiosity

Curiosity may have killed the cat, but it is a life force to the advisor. By training and personality, an advisor who employs wholesome inquisitiveness conveys a level of personal interest that enlivens relationships. Curiosity means many things. The nosey-curious person asks questions that seem to breach a level of inappropriate intimacy. For others, it is a form of voyeurism that morphs from being unhealthy to unethical.

Healthy curiosity, however, is a questioning mind as the servant of the advisory process. Follow-up questions, fueled by hunches, wonder what the other person meant. In focused conversation, this feline partner lounges in the room to question a response, ask for more information, or suggest a rephrasing of what you heard. For example, a client will often mention as an aside a funny or telling story from the past. Humor and curiosity can become powerful friends in a conversation. When a client shares something about her past, say, "Helen, I'm curious. When that happened years ago, what did you learn about yourself?" Now listen as Helen takes you where she most needs to go. In another setting, a client may share something very painful. Listen with compassion and patience. Then respond saying, "Tom, I sense that was a very difficult moment for you. I'm curious, how did others in your family handle that situation?" What you glean are insights into the person sitting with you as well as others who have shaped and supported that person's life.

There will be times when curiosity will be soaking in the windowsill sun, present in the room but unacknowledged. When a client reveals some intimate part of his life, give yourself permission simply to receive it without asking for more information. I remember hearing a story about the late Senators Everett Dirksen from Illinois and Howard Baker from Tennessee. Senator Baker was Senator Dirksen's son-in-law. When Baker was elected to the United States Senate, he asked his father-in-law for any advice he might offer. Among the many things Dirksen shared with Baker was this wonderful sentence: "Howard, perhaps you should occasionally enjoy the luxury of an unexpressed thought."[7] Not everything that can be said needs to be said. In practicing the listening art, come to recognize those moments when curiosity, or any words, are best left alone.

Creativity

Listening's third partner is creativity. Anyone whose work has an advisory component to it is, at the core, a problem solver. In my world, we solve clients' planning, legacy, risk, and financial challenges. At times, solutions are self-evident when we do thoughtful planning. Other times, solutions come slowly because of evolving personal problems that have no easy fixes. Though not said often, clients look to us expecting from us an imaginative solution. You may not have thought of yourself as being creative, but the nature of the advisor's work puts us often in that role.

Some will say, "I've never been a very creative person," without giving thought to all of the resourcefulness needed in a typical day in the advising business. What you may discover is that you are far more creative than you give yourself credit. Whether you are an accountant deep into an audit, an attorney wrestling with the evidence in a case, or a physician reviewing lab tests and patient history, imagination is at work by the very nature of your professional training.

Members of the clergy live off creativity. There is always a sermon to prepare, a counseling session needing wisdom, or an institutional challenge requiring guidance. Advisors, by default, must possess this quality. All too often, creativity is nudged to the back of our minds by the mundane tasks we do day after day, client after client, issue after issue. Like a plane's autopilot, we allow our work to become mechanical—almost robot-like. This level of our craft requires us to think outside the box as we imagine a different outcome by employing a new approach to solving a problem. In the mysterious corridors of the mind, when we listen attentively we arouse the creative process. Our clients feel a growing confidence in our ability to pilot a course of action. This creative thought exchange allows the client to hear her own words, often for the first time. Creativity is not so much a thing we have or do not have as it is a way of living. It is a mindset that refuses to accept at face value what is heard while processing the unspoken and unheard.

A few years ago, I was in a conversation with a gifted psychotherapist who shared his preferred approach to dealing with troubled families, stuck and unable to move through an issue to resolution. He explained to me that families, like organizations or machines, are systems. A father and mother relate to each other, and they in turn to their children, in routine, expected ways by virtue of years of living under the same roof. For good or ill, families and their systems can be both healthy and unhealthy. Recognizing this, he will schedule an appointment with the entire family, putting them in a room filled with five-seven balloons for every member attending that session. He then gives all present a marker and says, "You cannot come out of this room until you write one possible solution to your family's problems on each of these balloons." Looking incredulous, someone always says, "There aren't that many!" To which my friend answers, "You are paying me $150 an hour. I will be outside the door waiting until you finish your work. We will then look at all your answers and begin to discuss a way forward." He tells me they immediately get to work and soon have scores of possible solutions, each marked on one of the balloons.

For most of us, creativity has not been applied throughout the course of our work. It may not have been tried at all. If we are going to help the people who look to us for support, we must employ a resourcefulness that flows naturally from sympathy, empathy, curiosity, and creativity. When this happens, we find ourselves soaring with a fourth partner sitting with us in every conversation.

Intuition

In a powerful way, the first three partners now invite a fourth to join them in forming a virtual team. Intuition is the senses conspiring with the imagination to form an alternative awareness of all the data received. Intuition makes a deal with empathy and sympathy, creativity, and curiosity, gaining their permission to speak what none of them can quite craft into words. Call it a professional "hunch"—a voice shaping and challenging all the inflow coming into the ears and saturating the mind. As all these virtual partners sit with you, offering their wisdom, a fascinating breakthrough often takes place as intuition takes command. Remarkably, we discover we are doing our best work when these partners turn to intuition. They all hear the same words, but then our "hunch" in the room notices what I call the "meta-words" or the hearer's "What if?"

This hunch–aware of the barriers but supported by the partners—frames the data in another way. Interpreting the meta-words in tandem with the spoken words empower you, the hearer, to re-visit, re-structure, even *re-listen* to what you have heard. Put another way, this imaginative re-listening reveals the work of the subconscious in conversation. At work in every part of listening's labor, the subconscious becomes a wondrous and beautiful friend knitting the conversational pieces together. Aided by the subconscious, the advisor remembers the client's story already known while placing the present conversation in the context of that remembered story.

Here is where intuition finds its place and voice. The late Steve Jobs of Apple Computer wisely said, "Have the courage to follow your heart and intuition." Listening with the heart's imagination summons this silent partner for an opinion. Creativity yields to curiosity who then nods to intuition for the perspective words simply cannot express. This voice is anticipated and felt, compelling and gentle, whispering another take on the ideas gathered in the room. When we listen, aware of intuition's powerful partnership, we open windows on previously shuttered possibilities. Thoughts that once lurked in the shadows now stand in the light. Options unconsidered become viable.

In a powerful way, these four partners form a virtual reality team. As they sit with you, hearing what you hear, a fascinating discovery takes place. We have a breakthrough, realizing in a remarkable way we are suddenly doing our best work. Our partners hear the same words we hear, but they overhear them offering a hunch, a "What if?" to the conversation. This hunch, a servant of sorts, frames the entire experience. Empathy, sympathy, curiosity, and creativity, empowered by this hunch, call you to revisit everything you have heard. Disconnected dots link up, untouched meanings shake hands, and disparate feelings coalesce. Some would call this the work of the collective unconscious. Clarity comes, putting together the words and ideas, emotions and motives creating a potentially new reality. An insight comes to mind from the remembered client story. When summoned, it helps an individual see her life, and this moment in it, transformed, reimagined, accepted.

As these breakthrough moments come, an advisor sit as a spectator to their powerful effect. A client's eyes may dance with light or be drawn in with hurt. One word or image may scribble a semicolon that shows the client how best to merge his story with another, charting a new direction. We watch another think, and we listen rather than simply trying to get out the first thought that glides by our mind. The listening art reels us in when we rush to pile on words. What the client may need most is a sensitive but comforting pat on the forearm and caring nod of the head. Such is the transforming power of focused listening forging an advisor-client experience never before imagined.

All our good work on portfolio construction, risk management, and first class service is for naught if we fail to hear and see, feel and wonder, doubt and hurt for and with those we serve. Aware of the many instruments playing in the client's orchestra, all offering their music at the same time, we come to a unique place of understanding and counsel unlike any other. I am tempted to suggest we have lost the art of focused listening. Then again, we only lose things we once possessed! Like a master violinist or opera diva, practice and then implement focused listening in the symphony of your advisory work. Doing so will not only serve your clients better, but will create in you a person whose depth of care transcends the many words vying to be spoken when all along, all that is required is listening.

LOOKING BACK

■   Listening is the heart of a practice. It takes enormous amounts of energy and sacrifice of ego to listen to the words we hear and the "meta-words" our subconscious intuits from a client.

■   Barriers to effective listening are always intruders in a conversation. Name them, give them little quarter, and learn to recognize others that may be unique to your own personality and life experience.

■   Listening's partners include empathy and sympathy, curiosity, creativity, and intuition. These partners sit with us in every client conversation and give credibility to what we hear.

NOW WHAT?

1. Who is the best listener you know? Name three reasons why they listen well.

Focused listening is more an art form than we might realize. When you choose your best listener, ask who taught the listening art to him or her. Go deeper with your friend and make mental notes during the meeting to remind you again why this person is such a gifted listening artist.

2. Reflect on how you listen. What makes focused listening difficult? Are you distracted by inner voices competing for attention? How might you change your posture and/or environment to be a more effective and engaged listener?

Listening is a difficult undertaking under the best of circumstances. Opening my ears, heart, mind, and attention to a person speaking to me is work and may be for you as well. Enter every conversation as a quest to know and understand better and more sensitively the person with whom you are visiting.

3. Do you consider yourself a creative person? Give an example of how you weave creativity into listening to your clients.

Embrace creativity as a game taking place in your imagination. Visualize both sides of a conversation as friendly competition vying for attention. Find ways to compete on both sides of an issue seeing a problem or challenge from multiple perspectives. Give yourself permission to entertain an idea that may, at first glance, seem either improbable or even undoable.

Using this wonderful gift may bring a level of delight about work and joy in client discovery you may have missed. Imagine creativity smiling at solutions already considered and then give her permission to show you and those you serve another way of solving a difficult problem.

4. How would your advisory practice change if you became a more focused listener? How might you hear client stories differently?

Guard against being so familiar with how you listen and process what you hear that you miss being open to new client insights. Train your eye and heart, intuition and curiosity to be aware of the complete message another is sending.

Chapter 4

Learning to Think

The year was 1991. In a much-anticipated interview, consumer advocate Ralph Nader offered a glimpse into his life, his family of origin, and what he felt were factors that shaped his inquisitive mind. He went back to a time in his childhood and shared this memory: "One time when I was nine or ten years old," he mused, "I came home from school, went into the backyard, and my dad said to me 'Well Ralph, what did you learn in school today? Did you learn how to believe, or did you learn how to think?'"[8] That last question, spoken by a wise father to his gifted son, has haunted me for years. Perhaps for all of us, the temptation is to believe rather than to think.

Are we in danger of confusing what we hear and believe with learning to think, contemplating what is not heard? The question touches another application of focused listening as we weigh our listening partners' messages against the circumstances dancing around the conversation. Ask yourself: How does learning to think contribute to my becoming an imaginative, caring advisor? This question is not about our knowledge of the markets, financial, regulatory issues, or investments. Rather, it fuses learning client behaviors, attitudes, struggles, and successes with our own knowledge of self. Do you understand people well? Are you committed to learning to think about how your life intersects with others?

As a licensed securities dealer who holds insurance credentials or designations such as CPA, CFP®, CIMA, you must stay current. No continuing education, no license. Caring advisors absorb information in conscious, unconscious, and intuitive ways. We sit with our four unseen listening partners as clients teach us the lessons about their lives we most need to learn. What are they teaching us? What might we understand from this couple and their family who have entrusted us with their financial future? When the test comes, will we understand how they see life, what values they hold close, what fears they have?

Let us look at a suggested client-advisor curriculum and begin the "learning to think" journey. You will add other subjects to the syllabus, question topics I include, and with me scratch your head asking why some clients are easy reads while others are rambling, heavy tomes. Some clients' lives read like Tolstoy's *War and Peace* or Hugo's *Les Miserables*. You slog through every chapter, amazed at how these celebrated authors developed their characters and wrote epic novels with inconceivable detail. Other clients are like a John Grisham yarn: the predictable plot slowly plays itself out until you arrive at the last turned page where he pens a "Gotcha!"

We learn from clients experientially, conversation by conversation, year after year until at last we locate the key that opens locked doors. Some clients are more transparent—less cagey. These open book individuals may lead us to assume we know everything about them. Guard against such an assumption. You may overlook a detail in their narrative staring you in the face. Those missed snippets reveal a lesson as happened to me some time back. A client whom I had known for 25 years decided to move his account to another firm. I never saw it coming. He did not call or email to let me know; I found out when the electronic transfer hit our system. When I reached him on the phone and asked why he was leaving and did not let me know in a more personal way, he said he did not have the courage to tell me. I believed I knew him well, only to discover my failure to think.

The subsequent five topics address the importance of continually honing our craft as we lean on these trusted colleagues. As we guard ourselves against easy believing, we purposefully employ the work of critical thinking. Let us start with fear.

Fear

Clients may have more fear associated with their investments than any other part of their lives. Words like *downturn, correction, bear market* and *sell-off* send bolts of anxiety through otherwise calm and reasonable persons. Through active engagement, advisors come to understand each client's immobilizing fears.

Fear is a complex feeling to define. Physicians have told me organic chemistry is the subject that determines whether one has what it takes to gain admittance to medical school. They admit the class was the ultimate gut-check experience as they attempted to master a topic even the brightest find daunting. Fear is like that. A required course in life's curriculum, it traffics in nuance and misunderstanding. This feeling of dread is a tenured resident refusing eviction. Startle a baby and watch her chubby arms fly up and those bright eyes flood with tears. Have a driver ease into your lane, unaware you are in that car's blind spot and your heart triggers your hands to react as your foot slams on the brakes. Fear may lie dormant for a season, but over time, we feel its expression with cadenced regularity.

I first think of the fear of failure. Many accomplished people rise to levels of professional and personal achievement believing they do not measure up. My own experience with failure has been unpredictable at best. If you are a licensed securities dealer as I am, you undoubtedly remember sitting for that comprehensive, six-hour gauntlet of questions known as the Series 7 exam. Preparing for the examination at age 54, was, for me, a pass/fail reality as I waded into an unfamiliar ocean of complex legal jargon, market principles, and securities trading processes. If I passed, I had a job. If I did not, my short-lived career with a prestigious firm was over. The fear of failure was palpable.

Moreover, there have been times in my work when I have inadequately served clients, failed to meet their expectations or understood fully the problems they faced. In every professional setting, I have had moments when I sat in failure's uncomfortable, splintered chair. When that happened, I indulged in a brief pity party, brushed myself off, and overcame the obstacle at hand. While success has taught me very little, failure has been a formidable schoolmaster.

Clients who express angst need an opening to reveal their feelings. Listen with compassion as they tell you as much as their own comfort allows. When the other person has exhausted words, ask, "Can you think of one or two insights you gained when things were not working out?" The temptation is to deny failure's gravity or to refuse to be a student of its lessons. Failure has much to teach us when we sit in its chair. We must first squirm uncomfortably before we are able to rise and walk out of its classroom. To resist sitting there, even for a moment, may rob us of valuable lessons.

We also fear loss. Later, in Chapter 7, we will visit 10 types of loss. This dread associated with loss, however, can become an even greater threat than the loss itself. Senior clients have confessed to me the dread of relinquishing their driver's license and the freedom they have known for decades. To lose one's ability to come and go at will, of being alone, isolated or shunned is a sobering thought. Clients who live alone may need to off-load their anxiety associated with this fear. When you suspect any of the aforementioned concerns, your undivided attention may be the gift they need most to keep loneliness at bay. Maintain an active list of clients who live alone or are physically isolated. Call them more often. Assure them you are there for them.

We have a few widowed women and men in our practice. Some live alone; several are in independent living communities that offer security and social connections. Over the years, I have never called or visited one of these clients and not been warmly received. I think of Hazel, who lost her husband years ago. His death and the subsequent death of their financial advisor brought her business to me. After living more than 50 years in our community, she moved to another state and retained our services. I have grown closer to her and her children through numerous phone calls. I had no agenda other than to check in and hear her voice, and let her hear mine. When she says, "Thank you so much for calling," I sense from her a sincerity borne deep within her soul.

The fear of loss can be debilitating. Concern over losing one's job, even to an anticipated retirement, terrifies the employed, especially successful professionals. They ask, What will I do with my time? Will others still need me? Can I be around my wife or husband more hours in a day? Will I be able to make ends meet? How will I survive? On top of that, I am not sure we fully comprehend the fear associated with the loss of important relationships in and outside the workplace. It can be devastating, likened to a child's separation anxiety from parents.

Separation, divorce, and the death of a spouse have fear woven into them. I have heard divorce compares to death with one exception: the other person is still alive.

"Divorce is worse than death," said one woman to me a few years ago. "When you lose someone to death, that person is gone and you're able in time to realign your life and relationships. Nevertheless, with a divorce, you still see that person from time to time. When children are involved, divorce is like a zombie—dead but very much alive."

Though I am happily married for over 40 years, many of my clients have not fared as well. Some have remarried and now enjoy blended families; others are not as fortunate, having met an untimely end to their unions, bearing wounds they hope will not last forever. Perhaps this is why more than a few have remained single. Nevertheless, all fear divorce's aftermath having no idea of how life will be without that person in it. Be there for those clients.

The last fear may be the most threatening of all: that of financial failure. My work puts me in daily contact with persons who have spent decades accruing assets. Taking a risk at age 30 is quite different from feeling risk at 70. With this worry of impending financial ruin comes the prospect of losing control of one's life, options, and security. When my partners and I do deep financial discovery with a prospective client, we ask, "What does money mean to you?" The answer we hear most is security and power, two sides of the same coin. With financial resources, you have both. Without financial resources, you have neither.

A couple sat with us some time back to discuss their retirement. The husband had stepped away from a long career that had taken its toll on his health. The wife was receiving a pension after decades working for a non-profit. With her excellent pension, his large six-figure 401(k), and Social Security for both, they seemed amply positioned to make the retirement journey. As they talked, we learned they still had mortgages on their home and a farm not far from our community.

"My one fear," said Tom, "is that something will happen to me before we pay off the house and the farm forcing Gloria to sell one of them."

Gloria smiled, looked at her husband and said, "The farm is his toy. He loves that place."

We asked more questions and found the conversation coming back to the fear of investments being negatively affected. Our assignment was to craft a plan that would alleviate their worries and lay the groundwork for them to have a comfortable and stable retirement.

Learn to recognize and acknowledge fear in the lives of others. Speak to their concerns and help them share their feelings. Address your fears and ask if they are justified or phantom. Fear is often a powerful motivator. The opposite is brutally true: it can so immobilize you and those you serve that we avoid making intelligent life-directing decisions.

Trust

I have found this to be true: clients tend to work with someone they like, trust and believe has their best interest at heart. An advisor serves none apart from this expectation. Trust is the girder that supports the ever-increasing weight of the client's needs. Age has taught us, sometimes through our own failure, that trust built over years can be destroyed in a matter of minutes. We all know this, but how does this foster confidence in a cherished relationship that hits a wall both parties are unwilling to move beyond? What do we do when we are unable to reciprocate a trust? Why do we take for granted one person but not another? What do we learn about vulnerability?

How does trust work between two people? The image that works for me is the unwritten advisor-client contract. Once in agreement, we strike a bargain with each other that forms an imaginary handshake. We establish an eye-to-eye bond whereby two or more say, "I am relying on you." We inaugurate this tie, affording us an opportunity to insert a semi-colon, merging our life with another. At this early stage, trust is conditional. Like the other intangibles of life, all of us know when we feel it. A strong marriage establishes the promise "for better or for worse, for richer or for poorer, in sickness and in health, till death parts us." A deep, nurturing friendship strikes this unspoken bargain, yet it plays out as a carefully guarded alliance. When trust works between client and advisor, every nook and cranny of that person's life is shared: births, deaths, graduations, weddings and more. My partner and I work with several clients who would not consider purchasing a car without first giving us a call. That level of loyalty is a beautiful thing. This bond, built over time affirms the philosophy of life management the advisor espouses.

Sometimes trust hits a wall. When it does, what do we do? A small business owner once confided in me that his back office manager of fifteen years was exhibiting behaviors he had not seen before. Where once this man was rather gregarious and light-hearted, he became reserved, sullen, even taciturn and snippy. Innocent subjects like their favorite college football team or the golf affinity they shared no longer punctuated once easy banter. "It's like he's put a wall around himself. I'd try to scale it and break through it but I think he's way too fragile right now and I don't understand why."

Knowing this man, I shaped a story in my mind that seemed to support an issue of distrust between the two. I asked, "Can you think of anything in his life that could be troubling him?"

My friend thought for a moment and guardedly answered, "There was a left field comment he made to me from a few months ago that I ignored."

"And what was that?"

"He told me something about his brother who lives in another city. I've not met him and he rarely comes up in conversation. He not only lost his job but as a result found himself served with divorce papers."

My intuition was telling me that the brother's job loss was causing this man to rethink his own career and future. "Do you think," I questioned, "he's unknowingly transferring to you the uncertainty of what has happened to his brother, especially his employment?"

"I'm not sure I know what you mean," he admitted.

"When someone you trust throws up a wall, more times than not it has nothing to do with you unless you have threatened or broken that trust. What you may be seeing is a person who believes his own job is at risk, his own home is in jeopardy, solely because an older brother, who always seemed to have it together, is experiencing a bump in the road."

When the relationship seems fragile, look long and hard for clues. In my early years of pastoral ministry, I learned that some adults have huge trust issues with clergy. As children, they may have had behavioral problems that their priest or rabbi had to exact a measure of control over. No matter who you are or how you attempt to relate to that person, you may have limited success in bridging the trust chasm. Some adults bear gaping wounds from abuse; others grow up in households laced with cynicism. They have learned to question everyone's motives, without thoughtful reflection of their own. I am sure you know adults who find fault in the purest of things. As advisors, we are particularly vulnerable to this transference of judgment. An attorney may have been identified as the villain in a divorce decades ago and now all attorneys are suspect. A banker from long ago could have been the person blamed for a family's poor planning or lack of spending discipline.

Become a student in the lecture hall of trust and fewer obstacles will stand in the way of success. In its absence, problems become playground brawls, often without resolution. When others have trouble placing their trust in you, do an integrity check and revisit your values. With that personal report card in mind, remember that some may not be able to place trust in anyone, including themselves.

Take heed of whether those you serve are worthy of your trust. You may have a personality somewhat like mine. My mother commented to me when I was in my mid-30s: "Tim, you never met a person you didn't like." I received it as a compliment, but her comment, at last, hit me between the eyes. After further reflection, I found myself sinking into a dark hole. What I actually heard my mother say was, "You like people so quickly though some aren't worthy of such trust." And, like most things my mother voiced from deep wells of wisdom—she was right! Do not stop liking others quickly. Smile at them and enjoy the moment as they smile back, but weigh those first impressions with care.

Yes, there are untrustworthy characters who need the expertise we provide. Even so, I caution you to avoid relationships that emit negative energy. You might imaginatively place a yellow warning bulb in the forefront of your mind to automatically go off when you intuit a person unworthy of your trust. Nothing good comes from the inability to trust someone you serve. Being skeptical of a person, while trying to advise them through life's most sensitive decisions, is a formula for disaster. The nuance of trust is a precious gift. Rightly honored, we become its student.

Keeping Your Cool

Remember the last time you were pulled over for speeding or another traffic violation. Do you recall the police cruiser's blue lights flashing and sirens blaring as you glanced in the rearview mirror? With labored breath and heart beating forcefully, you pulled to the shoulder of the road and turned off the ignition. The officer emerged from her car, adjusted her Smokey-the-Bear style hat and slowly walked towards the driver's side of your car. You rolled down the window. In a subdued voice, she asked, "May I see your driver's license, registration, and insurance card?" Calmly, perhaps even predictably, the officer kept her cool while waiting for your response. Such is the training law enforcement officers undergo.

Capable advisors know how to keep their emotions in check as they serve their clients. Poise keeps us from raising our voices in response to a client who has momentarily lost his cool. If you find yourself at an impasse with a client, refrain from using inappropriate language or appearing defensive. It is unprofessional and counterproductive. In fact, when clients flip the script, we must remain calm, absorbing much if not all of their energy, so as to help them to regain composure and reconnect with reality.

Learning the fine art of self-control in the midst of a storm is not always easy. Lesson one: stay in your lane. Though unseen, there is an advisor mantle that rests confidently on your shoulders. When a judge ascends to the bench, everyone rises as a show of respect. So it is with the minister wearing the collar, the valiant officer in uniform, the proud soldier in fatigues, the able surgeon in scrubs, and the banker sporting a tailored suit. I am old school. It is my custom to wear a jacket and tie to work. Wearing business attire tells me to stay in role as an advisor. In an odd way, I find I perform my job better.

A child of the 1960s and '70s, I loved wearing wide-collared shirts and bell-bottoms. Casual was not only *in* but it exuded a style that gave texture to an entire generation. Life has since taken me in other directions. I have matured and so has my wardrobe. The week before I started production, one of my mentors reminded me that no one walks into a mid-town Manhattan bank on a Friday afternoon greeted by a trust officer in a golf shirt.

Though I may wear an open shirt and jacket on Friday from time to time, I never have a client meeting without wearing a tie. In professional settings, how we dress and carry ourselves telegraphs a fundamental message about who we are and the magnitude of what we do.

Second, composure grows in a person's life one appointment after another. Have you noticed that older professionals seem much more relaxed and at ease in their skin than younger professionals? When I was thirty, fresh out of a Ph.D. program, I was wound tighter than a three-dollar watch. I attempted to be all things to everybody: liked, respected, affirmed, and needed. This same feeling came to me again when I became a financial advisor. Series 7 and 66, life and variable licenses in hand, business cards in my pocket, and a list of prospects longer than most, I did not know quite where to start. Though language had been my currency for decades, I found syllables wrapped around my tongue, powerless to form the words I wanted to say. The more calls I made, however, and the more I asked questions and engaged the listening art, the more I found my professional center. Now with miles on the odometer, still learning from colleagues and those I serve, I see in the mirror a calmer, more self-assured person.

Constantly learn from men and women who exhibit what the French call *joie de vivre* along with gravitas. My guess is they are authentically at peace with themselves and their relationships with others. That centered sense of being, anchored to one's professional identity, welds steel into the foundation of your personality and work.

Authority

Learning to remain levelheaded in all circumstances now opens the door to authority. We have wrongly equated this strong, vital word with being heavy-handed, brusque, manipulative, even cruel. We are taught to rely on professionals who go about their work with a competence born of authority. We trust the mechanic to repair our automobile because we believe he is skilled at his occupation. We sign HIPAA forms that permit a surgeon to treat us. Parents grant permission to teachers to help shape the lives of their children. In every point on life's compass, we authorize and empower another to aid us.

Years ago, my wife had a terrible accident on one of her construction sites. That sudden incident brought us to the Emergency Room. There, we met a dear friend and gifted orthopedist, Dr. Randy Meredith, who attended Kathie's injury. He quickly injected drugs to alleviate her pain. Though our friend specializes in hips and knees, he knew the surgeon whose focus was the hand and wrist. Providentially, his partner, Dr. Joseph Rectenwald was in the hospital. Within minutes, he appeared in the exam room and assured us he would do everything within his training to restore Kathie's hand to its previous state.

When these able surgeons came to Kathie's aid, they spoke with us not as friend or stranger, but as competent orthopedic authorities who would bring healing and hope. In that moment, we did not ask to see their diplomas or what they scored on their Board exams. We knew, by their professional demeanor, use of language, and reputation they had the knowledge to fully repair her hand. In the months to come, healing came and our trust was confirmed.

Authority functions exactly like that in our work as advisors. When we enter a space, we must observe its power. We detect this in myriad ways, but most noticeably in personal hygiene. Frankly, it matters whether we brush our teeth, keep our hair groomed and skin clean-shaven, and have a pressed shirt or dress on. These fundamentals are on authority's team. With them, we have a good chance of winning the game. Without them, we have lost the contest before we have teed up the ball.

Your office appointments and the support staff with whom you work all exert authority. My CFP® certificate is matted, framed and proudly displayed on a prominent wall in my office. Business cards are embossed; my voicemail greeting is strong and self-assured. I wear professional attire and am conscientious about my appearance. Even so, such external appointments are only decorations if I fail to act as an authority. Associates who meet clients and speak with them on the phone have parts to play that transcend the submission of documents and management of compliance requirements. Not to belabor the point, but clients who enter our space, whether it is Monday or casual Friday, take in all they see: people, furniture, wall hangings, cleanliness, what they smell, and the way they are greeted. Those factors determine how and what you project to clients. These externals do not create authority. Rather, they shape the context for another, conveying the feeling they are in good hands.

Bear in mind: authority is granted, never seized. Thirty years ago, a wise minister told me that the pastor who has to say to his congregation, "I am the pastor of the Church!" is not the pastor. Conversely, advisors who do the right thing in the right way at the right time with the right people for the right reason discover how granted authority matures. Those who hear the magic question, "What would you do in my situation?" and its sibling affirmation, "I trust you" know they live auspiciously in the presence of this priceless gift. Clients have granted us full access to ask questions and raise the issue of value systems. When you have authority, you stand boldly in it. When absent, there is little you can do to gain it.

Not long ago, I attempted to carry a large box of purchases to my car without incident. It teetered back and forth in my arms ready to spill onto the pavement. A stranger saw me limping along and asked, "May I help you with that?"

"Thank you!" I immediately answered, certain my stack was about to topple.

She reached out, grabbed a couple of items and in so doing, stabilized what would have been a mess. In that brief give-and-take, she asked for and I granted her the authority to help me.

We do our best work when we get all the externals right while being acutely aware of internal qualities like authenticity and trustworthiness. As energies mesh, an atmosphere is established whereby others more comfortably and freely grant us the authority to help them. We fine-tune this consent as we learn how to use appropriately the rights clients yield to us.

Mentors

Mentors are a fifth, but distinctive modality. Volumes have been written, and more are being published, about the mentoring process and its outcomes. Your start in the business may have been akin to mine in that you enlisted one or more colleagues to teach you the ropes. In my case, my go-to teachers became my mentors and then my partners. As I reflect on our affiliation—how it began and matured—four factors played a prominent role.

First, they taught me that not everyone who appears successful has the ability to mentor well. The celebrated baseball Hall of Fame hitter Ted Williams still holds one of the highest lifetime batting averages in Major League Baseball. Seventh on the top ten list, Williams outhit the likes of Lou Gehrig, Joe DiMaggio, Babe Ruth, Stan Musial, and Tony Gwynn. He was a great hitter but struck out when it came to teaching his skill. Not every advisor can teach you her craft, although some may mentor you without knowing it. You observe the way they look you in the eye or how they phrase a sentence. You harvest what they do while indirectly learning how they do it.

The opposite is also true. Some professionals want to be thought of as exemplars and paragons of excellence, but fail the mentor test. When with them, you observe a lack of inner strength or weakness of character. Someone worthy of your attention must be a person you respect. In an odd way, some advisors become negative mentors. Your observations and intuition shout, "I don't want to be like that." Choose mentors who have a desire to teach you what they know.

Second, befriend colleagues who are successful in business *and* life. Sit at their feet. Watch them think and listen. Learn the questions they ask and consider why and how they ask them. My partners are, like all of us, far from perfect. All the same, they have strong and healthy associations and high respect with peers.

Shadow men and women you know who have strong networks in and outside the office. Learn from married colleagues who have loving bonds with their mate. Capture an advisor's wit. Absorb those in your midst who do not take themselves too seriously. Notice who offers sincere support when some unexpected sorrow shows up at work. Such are the persons you want to befriend and emulate.

One of my mentors is a senior client. He was a very successful salesperson during his five-plus decades of work. Tips he passed on to me are priceless. "Never say to a prospect, 'I was in the area and wanted to stop in and see you.' Offer a stronger invitation. 'I want to come see you! When would be a good time for us to visit?'" How about this one: "The happiest person in the room is the one talking. Find ways to persuade a prospect or client to talk about themselves. All the sales you can handle will follow." The last nugget of wisdom may be the best: "Always smile, even when you are on the telephone. The other person can tell whether you are happy, positive, and confident. A smile handles most of those issues."[9] This man was successful in business and successful in life. Seek out mentors like that.

Third, ask someone to be your mentor. This seems elementary but some advisors contend that asking for help is a sign of weakness. The opposite is true: the most capable people I know are intensely aware of their limitations (something awaiting our attention in Chapter 9). In time, you will become comfortable discussing with them any number of topics. One quality of mentor-ability is laughter. Mentors who have a robust sense of humor, who are not afraid to laugh at themselves, have an inner strength you want to learn. Asking someone to be your mentor pays a high compliment. If, for some reason, she cannot serve in that role, ask if you may occasionally turn to her for guidance. In 40 years no man or woman to whom I have put that question has turned me down.

Finally, master your craft and others will ask you to teach them. Mentees become mentors. This virtuous cycle is one of the best-kept secrets of our industry. Wall Street and its manifestation in advisory offices across the country are full of wonderfully gifted, astute men and women whose character and integrity are without question. Yes, there are the few who bring shame on the many. Become an advisor a younger man or woman will want to emulate. My partners' fingerprints are all over my life. I learned from them every aspect of the business, including how to retain clients. This type of specialized care has a beat, a pulse that invites constant learning. Be a student of the business, of people, of yourself, and of the nuances of client care and you will learn invaluable lessons.

LOOKING BACK

Ponder your commitment to learning more about clients and yourself as you:

■ Recognize and accept fear in all its forms.

■ Guard against working with anyone you do not trust, no matter how impressive the client may be or the size of her account.

■ Keep cool; remain centered and undisturbed. Learn to stay in your role at all times. Advisors must keep their heads when clients are losing theirs.

■ Authority is granted, not seized. You may do some of your best work caring for your clients in moments when you act on the permissions granted you as the advisor.

■ Identify one or two colleagues to be your mentors. Ask them questions. Learn by watching them interact with others and from the information they freely share.

NOW WHAT?

1. Name your top three fears. Does failure, loss of health or mobility, or financial setback top the list? How do you plan to resolve them?

Naming, voicing or writing down those things that strike terror in our souls is the first step to managing and living beyond them.

2. Make a list of the five people you most trust. What qualities do they possess that allow you to be comfortable in their presence? Are there specific personality traits they have that endear them to others? Are those attributes evident in your life?

A trust is an unspoken contract between agreeable parties. Become a student of those you trust and learn from them.

3. What has happened to authority in our culture? Why are we suspicious of persons in authority? Name three to whom you have granted this power and the circumstances surrounding each?

4. Are you comfortable serving in the role of an advisor?

Visit with a senior colleague who conveys authority in compelling ways and learn how s/he understands the advisor-client dynamic.

5. Who are your mentors past and present?

Make a commitment to identify a mentor and then ask him or her to be your teacher. Aspire to become a mentor paying close attention to how you conduct your professional and personal life.

Chapter 5

The Internal Storm

Anger may be our most misunderstood emotion. Strangely, we fail to name the source of anger in ourselves while quickly recognizing it in others. I have witnessed this phenomenon often. One of the memories seared into my mind was the time Fred sat down with me to discuss his mother's funeral. At the time, I was a pastor to him and his extended family. As the oldest child, now in his late '50s, he owned the company his father started nearly a half century ago. Their business visibility and legacy in the community was known and respected. His mother held the majority of the company's stock. He and his sister shared the balance. Mother and sister picked up a check and benefited from the annual profits. Fred, however, shouldered the entire responsibility of running the business.

Now mom was dead. The curtain was about to rise on a drama of Shakespearean proportion. From where I sat, Fred and his sister had to work through a number of issues. As we waited for his sister Patricia to arrive, I could tell he wanted to talk to me because he intentionally showed up early.

"Pastor, thank you for seeing me; I have to get something off my chest before Pat arrives."

Looking curiously into his eyes I said, "You seem upset. What's going on?"

He told me of long-simmering issues he had with his mother, fueled by his sister's lack of involvement in the business. Both women's expectations were to enjoy a large share of the company's profits. To make matters worse, not only did they vote on major decisions affecting operations, but his sister became a meddling presence with key employees leaving them confused.

If Fred's head could smoke, you would have seen the darkest, ugliest exhaust pulsing from every orifice! His animosity was visible. I gave him a few minutes to vent and unload much-needed resentments. After a while, I said, "Fred, we must continue this conversation after your mother's service. In the meantime, put in writing the unresolved anger you feel toward your mother and sister." I noticed his reddened face resolving to a more normal complexion. "For the next 30 minutes," I continued, "we have to plan a funeral. We have decisions to make about the liturgy that will make it reflective of your mother's life and legacy."

"Well hear me say right now before Pat comes through that door," he fumed, "my mother's legacy, for all her good qualities and the debt I owe her for raising me and staying with my dad will forever be tainted by the way she and my sister have tried to run my life!"

A few minutes later, his sister walked into my office and, for the next half hour, we had a civil, strained discussion about a funeral for the matriarch of the family. Two weeks later, Fred and I revisited the subject. With a bit of pastoral persuasion, I encouraged him to make an appointment to see a licensed therapist. Six months later, the business sold and he reconciled with his sister. Fred was in a much better place.

Unnamed and unresolved anger kills more people than are listed in the obituary column. It is possible to die without *die-ing*. We leave joy and meaning benched and ignored. Anyone in the advisory business has clients who seem perpetually vexed about something. It may be the government this week, the employer next week, children's issues a month from now. Avoid at all cost anger's toxic atmosphere. Remain mindful of the damage it causes when left to smolder.

Homo sapiens summon and experience instinctively anger and its many partners. When dealt with properly, it is a very healthy behavior. There are times when injustice or unfairness insist that someone express outrage simply to gain attention. When we lose a friend, loved one, or work associate to an untimely death, anger shows up as a normal characteristic of grief.[10] I have often observed the bitterness of a wife toward her deceased husband because he left her to face the rest of her life alone. Being shown the door after years of employment can arouse a level of anger heretofore absent in a mild, loving personality.

Expressing this oft-suppressed emotion over painful life experiences is not the issue. Failing to do so is unhealthy; it contributes to life-threatening diseases, chronic illnesses, and poor mental health. Complications arise when we are unwilling or unable to move beyond the source of our frustrations. I remember being stuck for days in anger's grip when a longtime friend betrayed my trust. She never knew—and does not know to this day—how misquoting me to a mutual friend wounded me and compromised the friendship. I was not free until I accepted that this woman was clueless. She was incapable of guarding a confidence or of being loyal to anyone except herself. Forgiving her allowed me to take the shackles off my life, setting me free to move into a healthier future.

Recognizing and Naming Anger

There are noticeable indicators telling us that anger is crouching at the door of our otherwise calm and normal lives. I mention three. The first sign is physical: the face reddens, the pulse quickens, the heart races, and the jaw tightens. Some, captured by rage, may even act out by harming others.

Our earliest ancestors learned to survive in the wild by developing an appreciation of their environment. This allowed them to flee from threats, both real and imaginary and to adjust to a mysterious and menacing world. Though a saber-toothed tiger no longer chases us, this fight-or-flight reaction shows up when something or someone threatens our safety or questions our autonomy. Though we hear and see with horror fanatics who charge into public places killing innocent men, women, and children, most of us physically respond to life's threats in ways that are more humane. We may raise our voice with a verbal blast, or retreat into a personal shell until we face the need to work through whatever has upset us.

Some years back I was speaking with a close friend who was going through a painful divorce. Though he and his wife knew the marriage could not go on as it was, they had found ways to make it work. Simple fixes no longer patched the brokenness after the children left home. Parents moved next door and his wife's multi-decade career ended. I listened as best I could as we talked. I asked a few questions, but could not get over the fact that here stood a friend of more than ten years who kept pushing his hand into my shoulder not once or twice, but multiple times. I did not interpret his behavior as a personal attack. Rather, his anger was so obvious he was compelled to physically place that pain on someone else. That day, I happened to be the one standing there.

A second indicator for recognizing anger is verbal intimations in speech patterns. Someone typically relaxed and soft-spoken who suddenly starts berating another may be reacting to unexpected bad news. The opposite is also true; an extrovert can suddenly become withdrawn or acerbic. Fluctuations in our resonance often signify an unresolved chord in our souls. The voice is not only our body's mouthpiece; it is a barometer foreshadowing an internal storm.

We see this in movies, on the stage, and in literature. Jack Nicholson's portrayal of Colonel Nathan R. Jessup in "A Few Good Men" stands in memory. One of the film's most iconic scenes shows the Colonel, known for his cool, losing it on the witness stand. Under intense scrutiny, his language, voice inflection, and face erupt in a barrage of vitriolic rage. We have all demonstrated the same, over issues trivial and monumental, as anger worked its way out of our lives in a verbal tirade that produced a hashtag.

The third way we identify anger is behavioral. Restlessness, hyperactivity, and withdrawal may reveal that the person we have long known has gone to the mat of wrath. Insomnia is also a key indicator. We wake up in the middle of the night and have trouble going back to sleep. When we dream, we meander through mythic and surreal scenes where we are threatened or attacked. In both cases, anger gets the best of us, thwarting our need for a good night's rest.

Adults in a committed, long-term partnership may notice life stacking on more and more stress. Anger is two-fold. On one side we are upset by what is unfair. On the opposite side we fail to get past whatever it is that has us in frustration's menacing grip. Visits with couples trapped by anger's grip have allowed me to offer a way forward. After listening to them air their dirty laundry, they often wait for me to say something. I smile and suggest, "When you are embroiled in a tense moment do you think one of you could say to the other 'Lighten up!'?" Humor used appropriately can be a powerful tool.

As clients sit with us, we must attune our sensors to the likelihood that the person before us is slogging through a situation oozing with turmoil. Some of those may look like:

■ Health concerns named, ignored, or unknown. The client simply does not feel good or suspects something is not right.
■ Issues with aging and the struggle to transition from one life stage to another.
■ Marital issues like loss of affection, confusion about love in one season of life to the next, sexual dysfunctions, and the threat of divorce or abandonment.
■ Employment worries induced by lack of fulfillment at work, loss of seniority, corporate ownership or management changes, and low self-competency as technology morphs from one level of complexity to the next.
■ Extended family stress as parents age, a child earns a degree with no prospects for placement, or coping with a special needs family member.
■ Natural disasters and housing threats such as flood or fire damage, neighborhood deterioration, and gentrification.
■ Spiritual doubts question life's meaning and purpose.

Decisions made by persons brewing with anger rarely turn out well. How then do we help our clients move through this continuum? What resources are available to assist us in this journey? And in what ways does anger consume an otherwise healthy person?

Moving to Resolution and Renewal

Recognizing and naming anger is vital if advisors are to help their clients move forward. Don't say, "I'm not a therapist. How do I assist a person who is in the grip of anger?" Admitting a lack of training does not lessen the importance of talking through unresolved issues which will better enable clients to make healthier life assessments. Please lose the excuses. What you must tell yourself is, "I am helping this person." We often underestimate our instincts and professional capabilities. Think about it. Your client is paying you a high compliment by entrusting to you a large portion of her net worth. She depends on you to address and solve challenging personal and financial issues. You have earned her trust. Stay abreast of the resources available to you and offer thoughtful assistance whenever you can. Believe you are making a measurable difference and you will.

Always listen to what, why, and how your clients are communicating. Take note of their body language and the physical delivery system in their voice. Have faith in your instincts. Ask penetrating questions. Progress is made when the other person is willing to talk and you are prepared to listen. When you give your client permission to rid her soul of whatever holds her hostage, she begins to heal. As you listen, acknowledge. When we do that, we grease the wheels of conversation. Guard the impulse to take lightly her frame of mind. Lack of validation is a slap in the face. It implies that her feelings are of no consequence. In contrast, when you acknowledge her feelings, you affirm her need to recognize the elephant in the room. Listen carefully and honor what is shared, remembering your partners sit with you.

Revisit the client's life story and remind her of how we are sometimes rerouted around problems that may, from time to time, keep us on the side of pain. Yes, life's passage includes moments that are unfair, unjust, and painful. But this journey also presents infinite moments of joy when we venture through anger and persevere.

Resolution is the beginning. The human ear, trained to experience music, tends to confirm what musicians call resolving the unresolved chord. Imagine singing "Happy birthday to you, happy birthday to you, happy birthday dear Mary, happy birthday to…" and stopping there without singing the final "you." Try it and tell me how long your mind will wait until you resolve the "to" into "you." Such resolution must happen. It is the nature of music and a fundamental principle of melody and tonal structure—the cadence of the soul. Unhealthy anger, however, is an unresolved chord. Its melody sounds like a minor, plodding, or attacking explosion. The voice may be strident and the face contorted. Anger that resolves itself in dangerous ways leads to the wounding of relationships, loss of health, and even death.

So how do we help our clients manage this tension? It has been more than 12 years since I became aware of the unresolved anger in my life over polio's discomforting sting. I was reading a book that dealt, in part, with grief. The writer noted that some losses in life are so far back in our past we only experience their results, keeping us from grieving the loss itself.

Because this insult occurred when I was 13 months old, I have no memory of being ill or hospitalized. Once discharged, I had to relearn how to walk while wearing high top, orthopedic shoes and a bulky brace on my tiny left leg, secured by a wide belt around my waist. Strangers dressed in white came in and out of my life. They poked my foot here and bent my shriveled leg there. My dad built a homemade railing system for me to work my legs in ways that were unnatural. This irreversible insult, though buried in the past, was very much alive because I had not named, acknowledged, and grieved the loss.

This chord of unresolved grief hung in tonal suspension over my life for 51 years like the Sword of Damocles. When at last I faced this life-changing deficit, my eyes flooded with tears that would not stop. I was a reluctant host, angry because a malicious virus took something from me no one could give back. When I released this anger that had seethed in my soul for five decades, a peace came over me that defied definition. That liberating moment shone a light across my story that exposed dark shadows and put other emotions in their rightful place.

As you listen for anger, ask your clients to tell you what needs to happen for them to get back on track. Our role at this time is not to fix their problem or tell them what we would do if we were in their shoes. Pause and chart a new course. Stay in the advisor role. Rather than offering solutions, be someone who invites the hurting person to verbalize options already considered. Psychotherapists have told me their job is not to counsel, but rather to invite from their patients what needs to be expressed. Clients who hear advice from their own mouths tend to move purposefully to resolution. By embracing the voice inside of us, we realize what we need to do and find the courage to boldly move on.

I watched this play out one day when a person with whom I was visiting off-loaded a semi-tractor trailer of emotion over the hurtful way his family had treated him throughout his life. His story had me thinking, "If my family had behaved that way, I'd have petitioned the court for a name change!" I listened and asked, "Marty, has the way you've imagined bringing closure to your family story perhaps always been an option?" He spent the next 15 minutes considering ways he could accept his past, face his present, and ease down life's road with a greater sense of optimism.

I questioned, "Which of those options sound most helpful to you? What is keeping you from moving into the future in the way you described?"

He shared the one solution I thought would be his choice. After a few minutes, his countenance softened, his voice broke, and he looked up to me and said, "Thank you for helping me see what was staring me in the face all these years." With one additional step, he saw and heard what his own mind and heart had already told him. I gave him permission to take the road he most wanted to travel because, in the end, it was the right course of action.

In the months that followed, I set eyes on a self-assured man who learned how to move from the toxic trap of anger to renewal. Do all conflicts end in resolution? Of course not. Anger unnamed and unresolved cripples one's ability to see clearly. Such a festering totally blocks the road to restoration. Failure to take out that barrier may lead instead to a dead-end with huge financial and life consequences.

How Anger Cripples Client Decisions

The old saying, "you can't see the forest for the trees" is such an apt metaphor to describe the toxic effect anger has on a client's mindset. When anger seethes beneath the surface, all one observes about the self is blurred or distorted. Mention the retirement planning topic with a client bitter about work and you are likely to get an earful of negativity. "Retirement planning? I've got to quit my job now before I go mad!" The person in front of you is so disillusioned by the fractured realities of the job he cannot think straight. This conflict keeps him from imagining the future and making appropriate pre-retirement decisions in the present.

Such resentments cripple our rationale. When we leave anger unnamed and unresolved we yield control of our future to a sinister evil that robs us of autonomy and self-worth. We behave as if we would rather coddle the pain than embrace the promise of a better future. In a seemingly self-destructive way, we argue that if we nurse the hurt long enough, the other person will feel it too. As others have rightly observed, bitterness is the poison we drink hoping the other person dies. Did I say this is crazy?

Frederick Buechner may have expressed it best when he penned: "Of the Seven Deadly Sins, anger is the most fun. To lick your wounds, to smack your lips over grievances long past, to roll over your tongue the prospect of bitter confrontations still to come, to savor to the last toothsome morsel both the pain you are given and the pain you are giving back, is a feast fit for a king. However, what you are wolfing down is yourself. The skeleton at the feast is you."[11] Distracted, we avoid naming anger. We may even be in denial. Wrestling it to the ground empowers us to stand free of its venom, retaining the one story that matters most: our own.

Yes, life by definition finds us traveling into and out of this fickle, unavoidable emotion from birth to death. For clients and advisors who employ anger management, the journey becomes qualitatively better. The caring advisor listens, learns, and observes, not allowing a client to bury the pain, sit on a grievance, or refuse to address it. Failing to care at that level of our work keeps us in a safe place but leaves the client trapped in a life of toxic upheaval, an internal storm that will worsen unless addressed.

LOOKING BACK

■   We experience anger in all seasons of life. Unhealthy denial or inappropriately expressing anger only delays healing.

■   We are wise to recognize and name anger as soon as we feel its presence.

■   Resolving unhealthy feelings is not only prudent, but our profession demands that we take up this noble work and help clients make better decisions.

Chapter 6

Stealth Emotions

Having surveyed the landscape of anger, let's shift our focus to other emotions we and our clients experience in less obtrusive ways. Meeting and naming these stealth emotions is tricky. If we think about it like a baseball team, we might better picture how they work. As with a baseball team, some players spend most of their time on the bench. Similarly, emotions sit in the dugout of our lives, always ready to play, but sometimes left out of the game. When a particular player comes to bat and hits a single, a stronger feeling may bring it home hitting a triple.

A second factor in understanding these emotions is gauging their intensity. We have clients who seem perennially disillusioned about something. In one visit, they find fault with the government or the President. During another appointment, they whine because their portfolio has a down month or one holding among thirty underperforms. Like a big beach ball forced under water, these families push down feelings until an upsurge of harsh words or aggressive behaviors violently rises to the surface. The phrase "I never saw it coming" has its genesis in relationships where submerged emotions assault an unsuspecting person. One of the assignments handed advisors is to distinguish between an outburst and the person's intent. They must draw from mastered life-management lessons to identify and interpret the emotional DNA of individual stories if they are to affect positive client outcomes.

These covert emotions often mask and protect a person's deepest desires but populate every life's team. They vary in expression, but in time, one by one, they step out of the dugout. Some send their best hitter to the plate when a bunt would be more appropriate. Others relegate these strong feelings to a corner of the clubhouse. Like the manager, when we read the play effectively, we will have greater discernment into the motivations of the players.

Happiness or Joy

The pursuit of happiness is universal, guaranteed in the U.S. Declaration of Independence. Parents want their children to grow up and thrive in a happy home. Lovers take enormous risks with their hopes and dreams believing the other person will offer them bliss. All will expend tremendous emotional energy, often with the grand assumption we know what happiness means. Who among us does not want to live in a state of perpetual ecstasy? Most of us enjoy moments of wonder, but few of us know how best to discover them. Perhaps we have confused occasional happiness with lasting joy.[12] Happiness is fleeting. Joy, on the other hand, endures.

Our clients bring to us their dreams and assets believing we have the wisdom and competence to help them uncover joy and purpose using wealth's gift. Judiciously, we guide clients through planning sessions, creating strategies that generate potential moments of happiness. That work, however, has as its goal the awareness that wealth used wisely creates possibilities that transcend investment performance. During client meetings, pose open-ended questions like:

- ■ Tell me some of the happiest moments of your life?
- ■ Describe what creates for you a deep sense of joy.
- ■ Who are the most loving people in your life?
- ■ Do you consider yourself a happy person? Why or why not?

For some, happiness kisses their cheek when they sit in a rocker on a cabin's porch at 6,000 feet. Joy, however, is the contentment found deep within the person seated in the rocking chair. For some, happiness is reading a good book; joy is the gift of imagination, lost in a story. If you know a client to be spiritual, it will benefit you to learn how faith informs her outlook on life. Pay attention as she talks about herself and her beliefs. Despite the charts, tables, and investment ideas you may have, conversations celebrating a life well lived are priceless. Talk about happiness, but press on toward joy. When we go there, clients are able to paint their own picture on a blank canvas.

Uninvited Guests

The place of deep helplessness in which we sometimes find ourselves may have its origin in *dis* and *des* words. Disappointment, disillusionment, disgust, despair and despondency are players that slip out of the dugout uninvited. We look up and, from nowhere, they stand at the plate. Much of life's trek is learning to work through curve balls and strikes. They come at us fast and uncompromisingly. When they do, we must choose whether we will freeze or whether we will come out swinging. No life is void of struggle; nonetheless, there is always the hope of a better future. The maturing person learns the temporary nature of all things and remembers that "this too shall pass."

From the Latin, the prefix *dis* means apart, detached, torn from. Therefore, dis-illusion is the emotion of having an illusion or dream torn from us. We go there when stripped of something held sacred. In a like way, dis-appointment is the tearing from us the appointment with our destiny, leaving us sad and dis-connected.

Another we confront is disgust. People who disgust us leave a bad taste in our mouths. An investment that does not produce the desired result, an advisor who does not lead with integrity or a financial firm that abandons its core values will leave clients repulsed. When clients express these "dis" words, getting them to talk about it is therapeutic. Since the financial meltdown of 2009, more than a few of my clients have aired concerns that beat a path back to Wall Street. They have voiced disgust and disillusionment over the greed of a few and the lack of sincerity of others. At every turn, my role was to help them express their feelings and listen to their concerns. We rarely win points when we adopt a defensive posture convinced we will change another's mind. Instead:

■ Look for hidden implications behind a person's source of pain.

■ Summon the courage to ask, "Have I disappointed you?" Be prepared to listen, hear and accept whatever your client says without being defensive.

■ Ignore the temptation to fix what has hurt your client. Your role is not to intervene outside the scope of your work, but rather to advocate for healing.

■ Remember that wearing the advisor's mantle requires a large degree of diplomacy.

Sadness

Years ago, I sat with John and Marjorie after the unexpected death of John's mother Ellen. She died instantly when a large truck ran a red light and plowed into her car. "Good-byes" were not shared between Ellen and her family. The promises and plans of a family's happy future died with her. To exacerbate the sorrow, John's father, Tom, had died from a massive coronary only two years earlier. His parents had been happily married 56 years. They were the glue that held the family together. Now, the couple seated with me realized their relationship was compromised by this horrific grief that showed up uninvited.

I convinced them to talk about their feelings; to tell me how their three young adult children were handling their grief, about their faith and where they had found strength in the mutual friendships they enjoyed. After some time, John said, "The sadness I feel never seems to leave. I go to sleep, wake, and meet it again in everything I do. My work has lost its joy. Our marriage, once full of passion is struggling. The plans we had for the future no longer seem to matter." What would you say to them? What can one say or do when sadness moves in?

I explored ways for John and Marjorie to move beyond despondency to restoration. "Would you consider working through an exercise if doing so might help you recover?" They looked at each other for a moment and then to me. Marjorie said, "With your guidance, we would be willing to try anything." I instructed them to take the next week and jot down as many loving memories as they could from Ellen and Tom's life together: children, grandchildren, and friends and how it strengthened their lives. They agreed. "Now," I said, "take the next step and write an imaginary letter from your parents as if they were speaking to you and your sorrow right now. What would they want you to know? In what way would they compel you to move through your grief? How would they want you to live?"

A couple of weeks later, Marjorie and John stopped by. They shared with me the most touching story of working through their grief. Having spent time recalling tender moments John's parents had known, they crafted the letter. Imagining Tom and Ellen's rich life with their family turned Marjorie and John's grief into gratitude. Sadness shows up in our lives unwelcomed, a rude visitor who cares little for our welfare. Time, memory, and imagination become friends who move us beyond sorrow when we revisit the past from another perspective.

Modify this exercise with any client when you detect sadness. Learn the names of loved ones in a client's life whom they trust to imaginatively speak to them. Often that person is a close relative. When we lose our voice in the midst of sorrow, disappointment or despair, summoning others to speak to us is often what we most need to hear.

Look back on your own life. When circumstances not of your choosing left you lost and feeling hopeless, who showed up? In my own experience, it was someone I respected who shook me out of my despondency. You may be that person to your clients. Never underestimate your ability to help them through the rough moments. When it comes to sadness, we will live with it for a season. Be one of the comforting voices that offers hope.

Fear

Clients live inauspiciously between fear and greed. Financial advisors learn this experientially. Someone has said that being a financial advisor is the only business in the world where buyers shun investments on sale (as in a market correction or bear market) yet purchase hand-over-fist when at all-time highs (a bull market top). It is in those moments of market volatility where fear may infiltrate a telephone call. A client asks, "Why didn't you get me out of the market?" The anxiety on the call has you picturing sweat dripping off the phone line. When it comes to money, each of us has a trigger that goes off for multiple reasons.

Clients often need to share their concern related to market conditions beyond their control. Couple their fears with a planned retirement and you will be at an impasse. In my 40 years' experience of counseling adults, three indicators seem to show up. First, as with anger, we may express fear in a physical manner. When we are afraid our heartbeat accelerates, our breath becomes labored, and our body wants to pace the floor. To say "calm down" to someone in a fearful state is unheard and can put more stress on the relationship. Often, time and improved life circumstances are the best antidotes to fear's physical manifestation.

Second, being afraid tends to mute sound judgment. As we noted earlier, our ancestors fought the foe or fled from it. When a client sees his account down 10-15% from one month to the next, his reaction is not to fight the markets but to flee them, asking you to "sell everything and put me in cash." We respond calmly, "Why now? Let's trust our managers to work through this correction and get us to the other side."

He says, "I want out. I can't handle it anymore!"

It feels like a fight, but the client is deep in flight mode. When clients verbalize fear, listening to reason or citing a respected authority strikes out. Fear and common sense do not play on the same team. The goal at this point is not to double down on our powers of persuasion. The best response is to be present to clients and speak their language. They need assurance. Our advisory role—when fear rears its ugly head—is to support them courageously and compassionately as the professional they hired us to be.

Worried clients require time to process what has happened, their reaction to it, and what they feel is their next step. Eventually they work through the tangle of their irrational thinking and behavior and open up to an idea or two that may help them better manage their feelings. Regardless of the source of distress, always validate the other person.

In every season, every life will know and experience fear. When clients are uneasy we must:

■   Recognize the physical signs they display as normal and expected. This is the body's outward message of inward distress.
■   Offer genuine support. Always respond to your client in positive ways.
■   Create the necessary space so your client can move ahead without pressure to make any decisions until they feel they are in a more hopeful place.

Ambiguous Kin

Uncertainty, perplexity, and confusion run parallel to fear. Individuals crave autonomy. Though groupthink and following-the-herd are sometimes necessary, mental health thrives when a person is self-actualizing. A friend acts in a way that questions a loyalty, a teenager goes down the wrong road, we stare mortality in the face and do not know what to do. Clients wrestle with the uncertainty of unemployment. Couples experiencing marital problems meet a level of perplexity unlike anything they ever have known. Investors suffer the brunt of the recession on their 401(k) and sit in prickly confusion about their retirement. How might we help?

The knee-jerk reaction is to throw fix-it phrases at these emotions believing they will put out the fire like a wet blanket tossed on raging flames. I was a well-intentioned, albeit naïve pastor early in my ministry, proud of my near straight-A seminary record. In spite of my benevolence, one church member set me on my ear when I offered her sanguine optimism after she lost her job.

Said I confidently, "It's going to be okay; wait and see."

"Wait and see," she roared. "Wait and see what—my kids go hungry?"

Loss of professional identity and job security threw her into the depths of perplexity that exposed my pastoral ignorance. My words rang hollow, void of tangible care. What she needed was a minister who would, in this moment of cruel ambiguity, offer empathy and support.

When circumstances break the hinges off a client's front door, use caring questions rather than insensitive one-liners. "What happened with your job in the weeks leading up to getting the notice?" "Did you see this coming?" "What signs might you have missed in your marriage that indicated a problem was brewing?" Get your client to talk about what is going on. Listen for comments that signal their need for a loving hand and listening ear.

Confusion, perplexity, and uncertainty invert life's equilibrium. We believe that all is right with the world, and the things that really matter are okay. Recognized for what they are, stop for a moment and have the client trace those feelings to their place of origin. Ask questions like:

"Did you leave a conversation having said something that wounded another person?"

"Have you slept well in the last few nights?"

"Is something or someone at work gnawing on you without end?"

Help clients do the investigative work. Have them express feelings that have barged into their lives, hitting them from left field. When they do:

■ Listen and invite them to talk about what is *back there* but unresolved here.
■ Resist the temptation to fix things with an answer from your experience.

We all crave emotional equilibrium: that feeling of being at peace with the world and ourselves. The best decisions we make come from tranquil moments and the worst when this ambiguity roams freely in our souls.

Surprise

Mark sat in my office and said not once, but three times, "I don't want any surprises!" The context of that admonition was a financial plan my partner and I had prepared for him and his wife. The Elliott's had created an attractive nest egg of investments including real estate, a small business, equities, and qualified retirement accounts. Their two grown children and five grandchildren were clearly in their minds as we discussed retirement lifestyle, long-term care concerns, maximizing social security benefits, and necessary estate planning. They were pleased and felt our plan was one that worked for them. Mark wanted no surprises. Neither do we!

Aah…the delicious emotion of surprise! Slip up to an unsuspecting friend, tap her on the shoulder and watch her jump. Surprise a spouse with a 40-year birthday party and you may get a look laced with daggers! Surprise an employee with a generous bonus and tears may flow. But surprise a client with bad news about an investment that did not work as you had expected, and the day may not end on a high note.

When clients meet surprise—good and bad—sit with them and witness a beautiful, raw response. All of us at times react viscerally. If you see yourself trending on YouTube, embarrassment might overcome you for a moment but leave you laughing for weeks. Catching a glimpse of this wonderfully intriguing reaction puts us in sacred space, seeing another unmasked and unfettered by convention. A client surprised needs only two things from us:

■   A safe place to show emotion
■   Assurance that you hold in trust these moments of vulnerability

Nervousness

Some people are jittery: they squirm in their seat, fiddle with their hands, twirl a pencil, drum fingers on a thigh. We all serve clients who appear to be nervous about something. I am convinced that nervousness is a way of letting out pent up energy. You may have seen the poster of the little, downy duck on a beautiful pond showing his feet under the water and his cute yellow body above. The caption reads, "I may look calm on the outside, but underneath, I'm paddling like hell!" We have clients who are otherwise composed, but fidget, drum and twitch their way through most visits.

In my experience, folks who appear nervous have been that way for years. It may have started in childhood. Parents put ideas in children's minds that may seem innocent at the time but have unintended consequences. Nervousness is often the result of negative encounters with others. Some really do believe there are things that go bump in the night.

I continue to learn more about my clients with every visit. One thing they have taught me is to distinguish general life jitteriness from occasional nervousness. We all have friends who are wrecks when outside of their comfort zone or area of expertise. In the same way, we know those who blossom when they are in their preferred environment. Some find centered tranquility lost in a favorite hobby or pastime. Pay attention to those times when an otherwise calm and collected man or woman melts into a puddle of anxiety. It may be a hint that something is wrong.

Here is an advisor lesson we are wise to learn. When I suspect a person's nervous triggers, I work around them. Meet with those clients in their world. Ask to visit their garden or stop by one afternoon when they are in the shop. To my delight, I have learned that meeting with nervous clients on their turf makes them more comfortable. In their world, I am the uninitiated and they the authority. Observe that environment and illustrate an investment principle or idea with something in their space:

"Investments start like a block of wood that, over time, become something like this beautiful and useful bench you've made."

The goal is serving clients, even when they may be ill-at-ease with themselves. It is for us to assess a mutual place of under-standing where problem-solving and decision-making can take place.

When I first got in the business, I was a bundle of nerves. I had the licenses and title but lacked concrete experience. Seasoned advisors instilled in me the importance of remaining composed when with someone who looks nervous. They taught me to stay focused by looking clients in the eye and to articulate in a way that may lower anxiety like, "Let me show you the simplicity in this investment approach." Having prepared for the meeting, outline an approach to a particular investment: "This investment idea is like a baseball game. We are going to play one hitter, one pitch, one run at a time. The market—or the opposing team—may seem like they have the advantage, but if we stay in the game, market history suggests we win. My role as your advisor is to keep you in the game for all nine innings."

We recently lost an account with a client who was, from our first meeting, a bundle of disconnected but obvious nerves. He wanted to get back in the market after sitting on cash for more than five years. He bragged about getting out before the great recession of 2008-2009. What he failed to understand was he had already missed a 150% rise in the S&P 500 from its March 2009 low. Now, he instructed us to put his money back in stocks. We asked questions about risk, time to stay invested, and aptitude for enduring market pullbacks. He assured us he was in. The longer he was in, however, the more intense was his nervousness in calls, visits, and emails. Finally, when the market corrected more than 10%, he called and said the inevitable: "Get me out today!" We did, he went to cash, and within four months, moved his account. Going over our notes, we did exactly what he asked us to do. His emotions, however, got the best of him. He, like many, had an inadequate definition of "investor" that evaporated when unavoidable market volatility moved in.

Nervousness is fear-based. When we work with clients who exhibit a high level of anxiety, we must rely on the teaching aspect of our job if we are to uncover some deeply buried issue that keeps the client from adopting healthier behaviors. We do not like to admit a lack of direction, knowledge or shrewdness but the absence of these qualities hinder our efforts to help an agitated client open up. Nervousness shows up in our offices for a myriad of reasons. When it does:

■   Remain in control with an inner strength and reassuring presence. Connect with your client and coach them around the bases.
■   Take on the role of trusted teacher. Use concrete examples to help your client understand a principle or investment strategy.
■   Anxiety is the outward expression of something buried much deeper in a person's spirit. Honor them by respecting their past and being a haven in their present.

Guilt

Perhaps the most pernicious of all emotions is guilt and its twin, shame. Words like ought, need, should, and blame haunt us during the day and wake us in the night. My parental self, unchecked, occasionally attempts to use guilt with my adult children. One of my sons recently called me out because I had wrongly slipped into thinking that I could use guilt to persuade him to do something I wanted to be done. It did not work. He called foul saying, "Dad, that approach isn't going to change my mind!"

Clients come to us with all kinds of remorse meandering around in their souls. For some, it is feelings of inadequacy in how they reared their children, lamenting choices made that, in hindsight, were not best for the family. For others it is financial and investment mistakes that may have jeopardized their retirement. Clients who face a cancer diagnosis may feel acute guilt because a lifestyle years earlier may have contributed to the malignancy. Business owners might feel guilty about the compensation they provide employees versus the success they enjoy.

Those who share a deep regret open a door through which advisors walk. Step over the threshold carefully. Human nature, without thought, can be found pouncing on the mistakes of others in ways that are threatening and disapproving. You must first take personal inventory. We have all made mistakes in judgment that did not reveal our best selves. The past is always behind us. What has it taught you? Who offered you grace when they could have admonished you? Have you forgiven yourself? Advisors who ask probing questions of themselves are better able to relate to clients immobilized by guilt. Take an inventory of your morals and lifestyle. Incorporate mindfulness in your practice. Tap into wellsprings of compassion as you walk through the door marked "Guilt" and be present to clients struggling with its menacing control. They will appreciate you even more.

Second, encourage your client to talk through the shame. Respond to his hurt with supportive remarks. Share with him a personal story and how you responded when humiliated or criticized. Clients are more inclined to open up when they feel as if you have walked down the same road. Guilt is a teammate whose best place is in the dugout. When this sinister player tries to take the field, exercise authority and get him out of the game. With our eyes on their future, clients will better manage their emotions and arrive at stronger outcomes for themselves and their family. Remember:

■   We all wrestle with guilt. Take time to name and exorcise guilt so you can then recognize it in others.
■   Choose to be a safe person with whom clients can share failures and mistakes.
■   Never use guilt to persuade a client to make a decision.

We are emotional beings and cannot understand ourselves or others without expressing a wide range of feelings. Positive sensations inject endorphins, dopamine, and other chemicals into our bodies creating magical exhilaration. Negative ones lay siege to our well-being, often leaving us sitting in the trenches of life. We must be intentional about identifying the entire spectrum of emotions present in our clients' lives. Every heartfelt moment shared within the walls of your office sets the stage for you to acknowledge these pervasive stealth emotions. Doing so paves the way toward healing.

Chapter 7

Advising Through Loss

Life and loss are inseparable. From the moment of birth, we entered a world of terror and wonder. Our parents witnessed the joy and pain of loss with every crawl and step taken, as we moved from complete dependency to budding self-sufficiency. Parents have told me they have mixed feelings when they turn to others to help them rear their young. For some, that moment comes early as a working parent returns to work from maternity or paternity leave. For others, it means making the tough decision to forego a second income so one parent can stay home to be the full-time caregiver or to homeschool a growing child. Through every phase of a child's life, parents experience loss. The first drop-off at a daycare facility is prelude to walking away from a classroom door as a son or daughter starts kindergarten. This "letting go" of our young repeats itself until standing before us is a high school graduate on the cusp of a life adventure that will ultimately lead him or her into an adulthood rife with the same joys and losses.

Many years ago my wife Kathie was outside our neighbor Sue's house when she noticed by the sidewalk a listless, days-old baby squirrel that had no doubt fallen from a nest in a nearby loblolly pine. She asked for a shoebox and an old towel in which to swathe it and bring it home. Others rescue cats and dogs. We, however, became the proud parents of a squirrel we affectionately named Goober! We used old blankets for bedding, bought bottles, baby formula, and began nurturing this helpless little creature back from the brink of death.

After Goober had spent a week in a large box, we realized he needed roomier quarters. Hair was now growing on his bald skin. He was coming to life in all his cuteness. We called Becky, well-known for nursing wild animals from sickness to health, and asked if she could advise us on a better living situation for young Goober.

"I have just the right cage that will fit on your back porch. Use it as long as you need it."

I drove our van to Becky's house, picked up the portable pen, and proudly placed Goober in it on our back porch. It was perfect! We continued to nurse Goober with love. We even put finely chopped pecans in his cage which he enjoyed. We would bring him inside to our family room and watch him scurry about, acting exactly like you would imagine a squirrel would act. Our children fell in love with this delightful creature as did we. Who would have guessed that a suburban family of five would have a pet squirrel? But that's exactly what happened.

For the next few weeks, we bonded with this adorable creature in ways we could not have imagined. Then, one balmy May morning, I went out to check on Goober and discovered, to my horror, he was dead. It appeared he simply went to sleep and never woke up. Our family was devastated. How could such an apparently healthy animal suddenly die without our permission! When Kathie and the children learned of his passing, we each found comfort in tears, hugs, and memories of a little life that brought so much joy to us so unexpectedly, yet so generously.

We put Goober in the same shoebox used to bring him home only weeks earlier, dug a grave in our backyard, and buried that precious animal with the same ceremony given a dearly departed loved one. The loss was profound, staying with us for days. With that experience, our children learned, and their parents relearned, that life and loss are equally yoked.

Our clients are no different. Like us, they revel in getting something new but are saddened by the prospect of losing it. Loss shows up as an uninvited guest. The challenge before us is to develop an emotional intuitiveness by which to identify loss in others. If you have chosen to be a professional advisor, you have perhaps recognized this as a critical skill, but found yourself unsure how to learn it.

What follows is a journey through the many expressions of loss our clients experience. You too live in the realities of gain and loss. This list is more suggestive than exhaustive. Linger thoughtfully at each stop. Give yourself permission to feel as well as to think. Become a student of loss in all its forms and you will develop a competency that will transform your practice.

NAMING LOSS

At times, we dance around a loss thinking that if we do not name it, somehow it will magically disappear. And yet, naming a loss is the antithesis of denial. Joan sat in my pastoral study some years ago deep in the belly of an anticipatory grief she could not face. Russell, her husband of over 40 years, father to their two children and grandfather of five, was losing his valiant battle with metastatic melanoma. I listened as she expressed the pain of watching her husband descend further into failing health. This, at last, was exacting a toll on her and the family. In addition, Joan served as Russell's agent and executrix. She faced timely legal and financial decisions which left her overwhelmed. After a few grief-filled minutes I asked, "Joan, can you tell me what your greatest fear is as you watch Russell's health deteriorate?"

She stared out my office window at a flowering Japanese maple and mumbled, "I can't say it."

"You can't say what, Joan?"

"I know he's going to die soon," she whispered, "but the words are like a noisy traffic jam stuck on my tongue."

Tears rolled down her cheeks. Soon an emotional earthquake jolted her soul as she found the words. "Russell is dying and there's nothing I or anyone else can do to stop it! I hate myself for being such a wimp about this, but he is my rock. He has been such a vital part of my life for so long, neither I nor our children are ready to let him go."

In that moment, Joan painfully named the loss before her. The words finally started moving from her heart to her mouth, allowing her to move from denial to reality. It was a first step in helping her face what lay ahead. Likewise, once we put a name to loss, we become open to finding resources that help us move through the grief to the reimagining of life on the other side of it.

Together we take this first step by naming ten common losses we meet along life's highway. As we do, pull from the recess of your mind times when you had to name one or more of these losses. Take mental notes, as we call on those memories later in this chapter.

Death

The elephant in the room of loss will always be death. Phrases like "passed away," "entered into rest," or "gone to heaven," all elbow out death: the greatest obscenity and life's starkest inevitability. Every life form on this planet has an appointment with death that cannot be canceled. I have been, over many years, with individuals and families when death showed her unwelcome face. Without exception, whether sudden or expected, we meet death as a menacing foe.

On any given day in your practice, the phone may ring and the voice on the other end informs you that one of your clients has died or is at death's door. In that moment, what words of comfort do you have to offer? The time to answer this question is before the phone rings. Early in my pastoral work, a seasoned, older minister met me for breakfast. Though we touched on a number of topics, the one thing I remember most about that conversation was the coaching he gave me on this subject. "You will not be a pastor very long before the phone will ring, perhaps in the middle of the night with news of a life-threatening accident or a parishioner's passing. Now is the time to begin thinking about what you will say and how you will respond." The more he talked, the more I realized how unprepared I was to pick up that phone! A bit embarrassed, I confessed, "No seminary course teaches this. Please tell me how you have handled those calls." I listened, learned, and remembered that morning's tutorial over eggs and bacon when the first untimely call came months later.

My pastoral mentor shared with me words and actions I pass on to you. When the news is expected, the questions and comments are always the same. "When did s/he pass?" "Was s/he home?" "Was the family there?" "I'm so sorry for your loss." If the death is sudden, perhaps as the result of an accident, heart attack, stroke, or foul play, you question, "What happened?" You dig for answers while trying desperately to make sense of something that, at the time, is hard to understand. Your goal in these first moments is not to interrogate the person reporting the news, but to offer compassion and a level of care that bespeaks your unwavering support. The most important questions you ask are not focused on what happened but how the living are handling this unfortunate change in their lives.

At times, you will ask, "What more can I say or do?" If you have a close relationship with the deceased and/or the deceased's family, visit them or express your desire to do so. Ask the caller, "Where is the family now?" If they are at the hospital and will be for some time, express that you would like to be with the family for a few minutes while they are there. Be alert to their needs. Listen with heart and mind and they will reveal your best response.

There are times when a client's death takes place in another town or state. If you are unable to be there, speak with someone in the family to offer support. Bridging the chasm of loss with sympathy communicates that the relationship matters to you, that you genuinely cared for the deceased, and that you will continue to be there for the survivors.

As I reflect on the lessons I learned from my older colleague and others that have come across the years, the best counsel is void of words or sanded down clichés. When a tragic event happens to someone for whom we care, we feel compelled to say something. And yes, I have heard the most hurtful, insensitive things said to the grieving. What do you say? The answer is simple: say as little as possible! Go where they are. Put your arms around them. Let them know how deeply saddened you are that such a loss has occurred.

Often you will take steps that demand considerable time and are no less an expenditure of emotional energy. Extend a helping hand offering to take care of some of the tasks facing the family. Options may include preparing food, chauffeuring family to and from the airport, making phone calls, and countless other duties. At best, attend the funeral. When we grieve, we seldom remember anything anyone says but we hold dear a warm smile or embrace. We remember the gestures that say, "I'm here for you." The clergyperson could be eloquent, the eulogy memorable, but grief tends to shut down the mind's retention of words. What we never forget, however, is the presence of people who care about us. Perhaps selfishly, we remember most those who show up in our times of need.

When death visits our lives, the loss is inexpressible, the pain devastating, the future unimaginable. As advisors, we have this moment in our client's life to be more than the person who manages her wealth, does her taxes, or handles her legal affairs. No, when this permanent end of life comes, we put down the tasks we are paid to do and we take up the work of the heart. When death visits a client, remember the following:

■   Find a way to be with your client's family as soon as you can.
■   Attend the funeral.
■   Keep words to a minimum but be present to the family. Express your sorrow in demonstrative ways.
■   Minimize your professional persona.

Health

The second loss we all face in life is health. From the moment we take our first breath, we begin the aging process. We all know people who live in the grip of chronic illness. When we lose some aspect of our health, coping with its implications becomes a daily challenge.

Clients who have lost their vigor, no matter the reason, need us to be sensitive to their situation. Though unvoiced, they want us, without pity, to acknowledge and support the loss. They may not need us to manage their financial issues differently, but they expect us to be aware of how this health crisis affects their outlook on the future. I have learned that being pro-active in connecting financial concerns with deteriorating health spans the entire net worth spectrum. Leadership does not need a microphone, but a steady, compassionate presence. In our business, having intentional, assuring conversations with those we serve clears avenues for even more important conversations down the healthcare road.

When loss of health is chronic and/or degenerative, issues like advance directives, powers of attorney, and cash flow become paramount. For financial advisors, questions about portfolio risk, sources of income, medical insurance, and filing for disability require not one but many conversations. Our clients expect us to have those difficult but vital discussions as it reinforces the trusted landscape groomed over time.

The common thread that weaves itself through all client loss is the need for the advisor to reach out in a more personal way. Call a client who is battling Parkinson's. Simply express "You were on my mind today. I wanted to see how you were feeling." No agenda, no business, no task to check off our list, just a call from one friend to another. Such personal, caring expressions differentiate you from others in your profession and convey to the client an unmatched level of care.

When it comes to a client's loss of health:

- Name the loss while affirming the person.
- Have focused conversations around critical issues.
- Listen compassionately.
- Make personal, non-business contact with a call or note.

Marriage

No advisory professional in our society today is untouched by marriage strife in his or her practice. Many advisors have experienced separation or divorce and know firsthand the pain such a loss brings. When a marriage dissolves, every individual in the family, including children, experiences a level of personal and emotional distress. Whereas adults will work through the death of a marriage, therapists tell us that a child may never give up hope that the parents will get back together.

Matrimonial loss can have devastating economic consequences. Financial advisors, CPA's, and attorneys advise each partner through the divorce. Assets, retirement accounts, and real estate will disburse, often by court order. One or both of the spouses may not feel you can remain objective. The process is rife with potential misunderstanding and distrust. Some years back, a close friend and his wife divorced. When I learned the details from mutual friends, my immediate reaction was fierce anger focused on my friend who would abandon his mate of nearly 20 years. His reckless decisions had jeopardized not only his marriage but also the future of their three children. Because we lived in different states, it was months before I ran in to him in New Orleans.

The conversation we had was one-sided, verbally sharp, and emotionally charged. I said some things months later I wanted to shove back in my mouth. Toothpaste, as we know, cannot go back in the tube! For his part, he reacted with amazing grace, absorbing my displeasure with understanding acceptance. His cool in the face of my anger said all I needed to hear. Some 20 years have now passed. We have renewed our friendship to a level of mutual respect and love we had not known before. I share this unflattering story to note that taking sides in a divorce offers neither party our best gift. What this man and woman needed from me was not a display of my righteous anger, but an outpouring of compassion for them and their children.

When a marriage fails, find a way to express to both spouses your commitment to be there for them in a neutral, non-judgmental way. Let both parties know you understand they may want to find another advisor during the divorce process or after settlement, but that you will do your best to earn their trust and retain their business. My partner and I have divorced couples who have kept their business with us. There were times when conversations were tense, but at every turn, we assured both parties that we would remain objective; that their privacy and confidentiality would be guarded like an armed sentry. Words, as we all know, can be cheap, but genuine attitude communicates and sustains trust.

When clients divorce, commit to each of them the following:

■ Independence and confidentiality in all conversations and decisions.

■ A commitment to high professional service standards.

■ A concern and advocacy for your clients' children.

■ Compassionate support as each spouse enters new relationships and establishes new families.

Career

Job security is one of the society's most oxymoronic expressions. Now in my seventh decade of life and in my third career, job security not only is a thing of the past but also a dangerous idea to entertain. The quickness with which employment interruptions take place impacts every client we serve and is a call to arms to advisors who take on any level of planning work.

It is important to distinguish between loss of career and loss of a job; the two are distinctively different. Loss of job suggests that you are a professional whose work with company XYZ is over because that business, for whatever reason, no longer needs you. On the other hand, loss of a career is a more devastating transition because the person may not have a skill set other than that one profession.

Thirteen years ago, I changed careers and began the process of reinventing my life and work after 25 years in the ministry. My education, which included a Ph.D. in New Testament literature, was solely focused on being a member of the clergy. At age 50, with my wife immersed in a new business venture and our third child still in college, I was adrift professionally and clueless as to what my next career would be. My experience is not unusual. Republished and revised annually since 1970, Richard N. Bolles' bestselling book, *What Color Is Your Parachute?* is a testament to millions of working people who lost their career, job, and passion for the work they had done for decades, or who simply wanted to find another career.[13] Thirteen years ago, I read the book, finding both comfort and guidance on how best to rediscover my life's calling and a new profession. I have recommended and given it to scores of adults who woke up one day only to learn their job and/ or career was over.

When job loss visits a client, we have an opportunity to be one of many life-counselors who help with transition. Because many of us wrap so much of our identity around what we do, work and self-worth, career and self-identity become one and the same. What question do we most ask when meeting someone for the first time: "What do you do for a living?" There are those who, in response, exaggerate the importance of a job in order to make themselves look more important. Women have been made to feel inferior as stay-at-home moms; men, on the other hand, superior based on their C-suite office view. Loss of career calls on advisors to be, for a season, a friend and advocate. Sometimes that means we share a client's name with a potential employer and at other times firmly steer the client in the direction of a new professional identity.

Clients will go through career loss at various times in their lives. For some, it comes early because of the financial constraints of having a spouse, small children, a mortgage and other responsibilities. Other times, as it did for me, it comes later in life when we may doubt our ability to reinvent ourselves. Having book-friends like Richard Bolles and personal friends whose names would fill this page, I found a new calling and a new passion. The passage was not easy nor was it without risk, but in hindsight, making that radical change of career was one of the best things I ever did. The fact that you are reading this book is a testament to my ability to cross-pollinate one career skill set (ordained minister) into another (financial advisor). Whenever or however career loss shows up, we, as advisors, can offer the following support:

- Remind clients of the gifts they have to offer.
- Give them an honest evaluation of their resume.
- Under-promise but over-deliver helping them find another job, offering our network where appropriate.
- Touch base with unemployed clients and find time to be with them.

Status

Loss of status is one of those intangible but stark losses adults face, often in midlife or later. Men and women who have known the exhilaration of breathing the rarified air of status fall from such a promontory devastated emotionally, personally, and relationally. As one of my senior clients reminds me: "It's easy to go up. It's another thing to come down!" Once you have traveled in first class, coach does not fly. Having the company credit card for 25 years is nice; paying for all your expenses yourself is a financial crisis!

When one of your clients loses prestige, reach out in a few simple ways. First, take a moment to write a handwritten note. Acknowledge your awareness of the loss while recognizing valuable contributions to the community. It has been a few years now since a friend retired from four decades in the banking business. Pat not only worked in the bank, but was instrumental in starting a number of banks in our area taking two of them public. A respected civic leader and man of faith, honored by his industry as a leader, my friend walked away from the only professional life he had ever known. When I read the news in the paper, I wrote him a letter, thanking him for his leadership, noting the many ways he had touched my life. Within days, the phone rang, and to my delight, I heard Pat's voice. We shared a bucket full of memories and smiles in the minutes that followed. He thanked me for my letter expressing how much it meant to him and his wife. We decided to meet for lunch, which we did the following week. Writing that brief epistle took ten minutes and a first class stamp. The dividends we still share will last a lifetime!

Second, wait a few days after mailing the note to give the person a call inviting them to dine out. When loss comes, sharing a meal is like a warm blanket on a very cold night. Literature and history abound in illustrations that show the power of breaking bread with someone going through a tough time. Make that call. Schedule a visit over good food. While together, find a way to get the person to talk about his loss. If the person was terminated or involuntarily retired, sharing details may be very painful. By inviting the person to talk out the loss, you again affirm your care for the person. Your role is not to agree or disagree with what happened as much as it is to be a listening, supportive, and caring friend.

Then, as months wear on, find a way to enlist memory as your partner. You could, in passing, say to the past president of your civic club, "Last year was one of the finest in our club's history." The retired school principal you run into at the grocery store will dance through the remainder of her day because you said, "Our children could not have had a better education on your watch." The minister, priest, rabbi, or congregational leader whose gifts blessed you and your family will stand a bit taller in their later years because you seized the perfect moment to say, "I cannot imagine how impoverished my life would have been without you in it." Leadership can be a lonely office. Look for ways to express gratitude to those who occupied a once lofty position whose soul will take flight because you said "thank you."

There is not a person given status at any level of life that does not mourn its loss when change comes. As advisors you can offer the following:

■   Reach out as soon as you know about the loss and write that note.
■   Pick up the phone and invite the person to join you for a meal.
■   Be a safe person who listens to your clients' pain while affirming them and their gifts as a leader.

Friendship

One of the lessons from childhood on is the unavoidable loss of friendship. As children, we learn friendship's dynamics in many ways through the experience of loss. Being mean (in all its manifestations) is not a good tool to build friendships. Likewise, the boy or girl who embarrasses, bullies, or ignores us sooner or later becomes a non-friend. By the time we reach high school, friendships start to solidify into life-long relationships that rekindle at class reunions after 10, 20, and 50-years.

Not all friendships last. Some relationships are so thinly bonded they probably need to die. Others ebb and flow with the changing tides of family, business, community, and faith. One doesn't have to live long to experience the devastating loss of a good friend. Some friendships are lost to death, others to betrayal, and more than a few to neglect. Some are lost for no other reason than your lives going in different directions. You by now have heard the saying, "Some friends are for a season, some for a reason, others for a lifetime."

In April 1990, Kathie and I along with our three children moved from Tuscaloosa, Alabama to Augusta, Georgia. Our oldest son was 11, about to finish the fifth grade. We knew the move would be hard on all three of our children, but something in my soul told me I needed a private moment to share the news with Nathan. It was a Saturday morning when the two of us got in the car to run some errands. Sitting in the parking lot of Lowe's, I told Nathan there was a church in Augusta that had called me to be their pastor and we would be moving. He looked at me with tears on his cheeks and said, "Dad, how can we leave all our friends in Tuscaloosa? I don't want to leave." Then I cried. Together, we shared our grief knowing our family would be saying good-bye to people we dearly loved. And yes, our Tuscaloosa friends would know a similar grief as they said good bye to us.

Reflecting on that moment in our shared lives many years ago reminds me again of this powerful, binding reality we call friendship. Take a moment to reflect on the friendships you have treasured and those you have lost. Could you have done more to keep the ones you no longer have? Is there a lost friendship you would like to rekindle? What traits can you identify in yourself that you look for in others? What is the common thread that weaves itself through your lasting relationships, as well as those that end?

Answering those questions will give you greater insights into the bonds you forge with clients. Though some in the advisory role do their work at arm's length, I for one have found the distant approach to business both unsatisfying and artificial. Clients entrust to us not only their business but also their futures. When we show up in their lives concerned and connected, friendship forms. It is a natural evolution of care. When clients leave our practice for any reason, we feel the loss because, over time, relationships were nurtured that allowed us to support and benefit their lives and the lives of their families.

But what happens when loss of friendship shows up in your office as a business problem? What do we do when friends who are business partners decide their grand idea a few years ago to create a company together no longer works? And where do we stand when professionally we serve two individuals who have fallen out with each other with no hope of reconciliation?

In my 25 years of pastoral work, I have witnessed firsthand the aftermath of emotional scarring when great friendships die. Often such a loss will bleed over to spouses, children and extended family. Business partners who call it quits with each other may resort to litigation that is both expensive and destructive. When loss of friendship comes to us personally or in the lives of those we serve, we may be able to weather the storm by keeping in mind the following truths.

First, our lives are enriched by friends and at times defined by them, but they are not lived through them. When a friendship is healthy, each person's life is enriched and ennobled. Sometimes, a friendship becomes dysfunctional because one or both parties attempt to live their lives through the other. As a result, self-worth becomes associated with how a friend feels about us rather than how we feel about ourselves. Issues with people outside the relationship can poison the friendship unawares. Toxic behaviors, be it irresponsible moral failure or illegal lifestyle choices, find an open door and soon destroy everything in their path. Remember that friends are wonderful gifts but often poor definers of our lives.

Second, friendship works only when both persons acknowledge that it is thriving but vulnerable. Years ago I made a life-long friend in Bill Curry. At the time we met, Bill was head football coach at Alabama. Later he went to Kentucky and then for more than a decade was an analyst for ESPN. When we first met, Bill and I were both in a place professionally where we found strength in each other's presence. I will never forget when, early in the friendship, he said to me, "Tim, let's see where this goes and enjoy our time together for as long as it works." Over time, we've shared conversations, laughs, and hugs. Our friendship has now worked for nearly 30 years!

Like every living thing in the cosmos, friendships are born and ultimately die. When clients go through the loss of a friendship, they experience death in a profoundly painful and personal way. Our gift to clients when loss of friendship shows up in conversation is to help them bring to mind all the good the friendship produced over the years. Help your client focus on the positive life-enriching history rather than the sudden, painful end.

So as advisor, remember we can respond to the loss of friendship.

■   Be true to the definition of who you are.
■   Accept friendship's vulnerable side while doing your part to make it work.
■   Acknowledge that friendships ultimately die but even when they do, you often take good memories with you.

Children

From a child's conception, we embark on a trip that will lead to a loss. The moment we hold our own child in our arms, the sacred enters into two lives. A wonder of wonders occurs. It is love at first sight. Once you are a parent, you are a parent for life. That is an unchanging fact. Children soon conform to the ways of their caretakers; the wheel of life revolves, through infancy, adolescence, and young adulthood. One of the obvious ways in which we lose our children is through the process of maturation. An infant becomes a toddler, a toddler becomes a preschooler, a preschooler enters kindergarten, then elementary, middle school, high school, college and beyond. We lose our children to caregivers, teachers, playmates, first crushes, and then to complete strangers who steal their hearts. We then lose them to careers and colleagues, spouses and children, in-laws and therapists. At last, we lose them to their own ideals. This circle of gains and losses impacts families in profound ways.

One day a client is going to be visiting with you when the topic turns from a planning issue to the loss of a child. You may learn there was a stillborn baby or a miscarriage years ago with the grief still lingering as a brutally incomplete sentence. Be mindful that as a parent, there is no greater loss than the death of a child. Years back, a group of young people was at our home for a summer Bible study. For two hours, the walls hummed with dozens of teenagers. When the meeting ended, we walked a couple who were dating to the front door, hugged them both, and said "Good night. See ya Sunday morning." Less than 20 minutes later, the young lady, sitting in the passenger seat, absorbed a lethal blow as an SUV plowed into the car her date was driving. The phone rang with news of the accident. In unspeakable shock, Kathie and I got in the car and drove to the medical school's trauma unit where, in the wee hours of the next morning, this precious young life ended.

The next several days are somewhat of a blur. Life seemed to stop for all of us. A loving church gathered around her mother and father, her three sisters, and a community whose broken hearts beat faintly with grief. As I prepared for her memorial service, asking for wisdom beyond my years and training, a layperson asked me, "How do you preach the funeral for a 17 year old?" My answer came from a big lump in my throat. "I don't know, but one funeral for a teenager in your entire ministry is one funeral too many." The loss of that beautiful young life forever changed her family and all of us who knew her. There is no greater loss or unending soul sorrow than to lose a child to death.

A loss of far less magnitude comes when parents learn their children are moving into the world with their own ideas about life and its meaning. A wise person shared with me nearly 15 years ago, as our children were making their way through college, that Kathie and I had best accept the fact that the dreams we have for our children are not the dreams they have for themselves. My heart tells me I do my best parenting by tossing in history's waste basket those old weathered dreams needing to die so as to take up the living dreams in the hearts of those we call our offspring.

The great majority of our clients, however, will lose their children in the natural unfolding of maturity. How do we connect with clients in this season of their lives? First, acknowledge their frustrations and any other feelings they share. Next, remind them that every parent has gone through similar experiences with their children. Then, perhaps humorously suggest to them that this is what they signed up for when they brought children into this world. Help them see that the positive life path their child has chosen is an affirmation of their disciplined and loving child-rearing skills. Parents will always be parents. The guiding, nurturing, and protecting behaviors we exhibit are, all together, tools whereby the child grows up and becomes independent. For each to know such wholesome, forward-looking autonomy is the goal of every father and mother.

Remain sensitive to the loss of a child to illegal or immoral lifestyle choices. We may have a client who has an irresponsible child lost to a crippling addiction or involved in an abusive relationship. Parents who lose a child to the dark side of human nature have a unique and at times embarrassing hurt that is often hard to share. Offer your support by first acknowledging the parent's concerns; second, by showing concern for the child in a non-judgmental way. Exhibiting a gentle hand in matters of the heart will help you forge a bond with clients that far surpass your advice and is in itself worth its weight in gold.

As we work with clients through the loss of children to independence and adulthood, keep in mind:

■　Children leave the nest. Parental separation anxiety in this life transition is normal and expected.

■　Children who transition to adulthood with purpose bear witness to the good gifts parents gave them.

■   Some clients' children are lost to behaviors and lifestyles that are unhealthy and dangerous. Listen, support, and be non-judgmental.

Community

We are a mobile society. Gone are the days when most families enjoy a "Walton's Mountain" experience where multiple generations live near or with each other. Children grow up and leave home, neighbors change, businesses close and relocate, stores liquidate, schools decay. Certain losses show up with regularity. The first is a loss of community to demographic or economic change. This systemic decline has a direct impact on our relationships with clients. Recent news of Detroit's financial challenges has pundits and residents alike searching for reasons for its slump. Detroit lost its neighborhoods. Upwardly mobile adults moved to the suburbs in droves. The auto industry faced its own set of challenges. Layoffs ensued. Homes were abandoned, yards unkempt. Other American cities face similar challenges.

There are clients who have chosen to stay in the home in which they reared their children even though their neighborhood has experienced severe decay. They have the money to relocate, but emotional ties to that which is familiar hold them in a grip that logic and security will not loosen. If you have a client who is facing this type of community loss, speak with them. Speak to good memories from years gone by while raising questions about security, home values, and plans the city may have to either revitalize or radically change the area.

A second loss shows up in relationships formed within a close community. As we age, being a part of a nurturing, sustaining locale is vital to our mental and physical health. Human beings need interaction with one another. Living alone or isolated from those you hold dear can contribute to the early onset of mental health issues like dementia and Alzheimer's disease.

This same loss also shows up in the connections we enjoy with people in social clubs, houses of worship, and affinity groups, all of which hold themselves together through the magic of community. When someone loses even one of these cherished relationships because of failing health, grief rears its troubling head. Equally overwhelming is when aging parents must uproot themselves from beloved neighborhoods and lifelong friends to move hundreds of miles away so children can better care for them. This change in life is often devastating.

The third loss of community is identity. When you tell someone you are a Rotarian, all kinds of good feelings manifest themselves. Being a part of a community of faith, a colony of artists, a center of friends or sports enthusiasts imprints a unique identity on a life unlike any other. Perhaps like me you have a healthy identity as a musician, a bridge player, or a church member. As a senior, however, loss of that identity in community leaves us redefining a part of our personality when time is not on our side.

When a client goes through some loss of community, advisors will want to be especially sensitive to painting too optimistic a picture of changes that may await the person in another place. Shutting off the freedom to grieve, to express disappointment, and to name loss diminishes the value of the community the person is giving up. Give them space to talk out their loss and even vent their anger. Then assure your client you will continue to be there for them regardless of where they relocate. We have a client who, in the last year, has moved 800 miles away to another state. I make it a point to call her more now than I did when she lived in our community. We talk about mutual friends. She asks about news from the retirement community where she once lived among friends who have since fallen ill or died. Community is all about relationships. When we lose community, part of us dies while the other part wonders if life will ever be the same.

Loss of community affects us all at some time in our lives. When that happens with our clients:

■ Give them permission to express their grief.

■ Assure them of your continued interest and care.

■ Follow up often. Maintain the relationship by not only checking on your client but by putting names to events in the community with which they can relate.

Passion

There are times when we lose the joy of living. It plods out of the room taking with it the light of morning's promise and the hope beyond day's end. Many know the emptiness of a passionless, joyless life. I am not talking about clinical depression which shows up as bipolar disorder or other mental illnesses. Nor am I referring to periodic disappointments that come and go as we meet the challenges of work, family, and community responsibilities.

The loss of passion I refer to is what the ancient mystics called "ennui": lethargy, sloth, cynicism, despondency. Thomas Aquinas labeled sloth as one of the Seven Deadly Sins. Ennui is its kin, suggesting that nothing matters. Loss of passion is a life killer because it intimates that we have nothing to offer. Even if we did, our offering would not make a bit of difference to anyone for any reason.

Years ago I sat with a client who was going through this passion malaise. Midlife with more than a few compelling personal and professional talents, this man had hit a career dead-end. He was losing his mental health, literally shutting down with his wife, friends, and family. When we met for lunch, he was at rock bottom. There was no light in his eyes, no vigor in his voice, no promise in his future so far as he could tell, although I heard hints of a word here and there that told me he would work through this in time. All I could do was listen. A strong faith and supportive spouse gave him the needed strength to move through this season. Although there was no silver bullet that day, my friend has since reinvented his professional life and is enjoying uncommon success.

When clients or friends find themselves in this place where passion for life seems lost, find a way to be with them privately. Get them to talk about their fears, anger, disappointments…all the reasons they can name for shutting down. Some of you may even be aware of a time in your life where you faced something similar. What happened to you that turned the tide toward optimism? Share with him that story.

Many years ago I lost enthusiasm for the work I once loved. My mother, now of blessed memory, listened to me vent, then offered me sage advice: "Tim, never forget that in any situation in life, you have more going for you than you have going against you." Mom was right. Loss of passion is crippling for many reasons, not the least of which it suggests there is no hope for a better tomorrow.

Advisors have the opportunity to share with clients that hope is not dead unless we choose to kill it. As Richard Bolle reminds his readers, discovering what makes us tick—not others' definition, but ours—awakens new life, energy, and direction. Clients may lose passion for work, passion in their marriage, passion for a hobby, passion for learning, or passion for travel. Our offering to clients in this season of loss is to help them rediscover the spark that makes them the uniquely wonderful person they are.

So as you sit with someone who has lost passion in life, help them by:

■   Investing in one-on-one time to remind them they are a person of worth.
■   Sharing your own journey from loss to rediscovery of passion.
■   Spending as much time as you can with them to help them move forward.

Faith

The tenth loss our clients face is faith. Lest you think this minister-advisor is referring to the loss of religious faith, such is not the case. This loss may happen to a person whose beliefs have been steadfast; consequently, losing one's faith can have wounding outcomes. My sense is that some of the people we serve today have lost their faith in many of the structures of our society and culture. There is more division today in Washington than I can remember in my lifetime. Compromise is lacking in members of both parties, while courage has seemingly disappeared. American citizens lack confidence that local and national leadership can steer the country in the right direction. State and local politicians struggle to hear the voices of their constituents. Cities are being torn apart because some believe the justice system is broken. More than a few no longer trust the police.

At times, clients who sit before us are not sure they can place their faith in us. The financial services industry where I find my practice has known more than a few scandals involving insider trading, money laundering, and broker indiscretion. Every time we are with clients, we need be aware they are evaluating us. Once faith is lost in a person or an institution, it is hard to win back. As we serve clients, always be mindful that integrity is our only currency.

How do you help someone who has lost faith in another person, an institution, or even an ideal? One thing we must do is to listen for inaccurate language. The 24/7 news cycle suggests that a problem in New York City is a problem in every city in the United States. "They're all crooks in my book" is a scathing indictment that cannot be left unchallenged. You are not a crook nor am I. We practice our advisory craft with integrity, remaining faithful to the principles of our profession. When one of our number falls, we expect the authorities to bring a swift action to those who abuse the public's trust. When someone makes a blatantly untrue statement, firmly call them out asking, "Do you think I'm a crook?" Or, "Do you believe I would work for a company that had no sense of morality or integrity?"

Second, listen for other issues that have little or nothing to do with what is being addressed by your client. I have learned in my pastoral work and now as a financial advisor that the junk that shows up in my office often has little to do with me or the firm for which I work. When someone acts out in anger, suspicion or contempt of others, there is often something going on far more troubling. What is behind the loss of faith that may be unexpressed or unnamed?

Last, always act with integrity, doing the right thing in the right way for the right reason with the right people at the right time. Give your clients no reason to lose faith in you. Rather than telling them how trustworthy you are, be trustworthy. Be the person you would want to manage your mother's portfolio. Convey to the person whose faith has been lost that there continue to be people in this world who will not disappoint them.

Loss of faith seems epidemic in our society. Our advisory work calls us to:

■   Help clients use language accurately lest they categorize all advisors with the small minority who abuse the public's trust.
■   Be a trusted person who acts responsibly.
■   Listen to other issues that may be the source of your client's loss of faith.
■   Act with integrity.

Life and loss are inseparably bound to each other. We will enjoy as well as lose life's abundant treasures. One day, we will experience the loss of our own life to death. The sun rises and sets on our stories in mysterious yet wonderful ways. We must learn to live with the phenomenon of loss as a natural aspect of a transient life. In so doing, we are better equipped to help our clients cope during their seasons of loss, as they move again toward hope.

Chapter 8

Nurturing Presence

To excel in a successful advisory practice, you must develop a broad understanding of markets, risk assessment, planning, and other competencies. However, to exceed client expectations beyond portfolio management, you must have a caring presence clothed with authenticity. A man or woman whom people like, trust, and believe has their best interest at heart will benefit from a long list of satisfied clients over the one whose practice is egocentric. This moral soundness that few in the business talk about has at its center the power of a nurturing presence. Although difficult to define, we know when we are with persons who have it because they exude a level of confidence that draws us to them. Individuals who have met the President of the United States express this when meeting the nation's chief executive. Similarly, advisors aware of this connecting force create an undeniable effectiveness within their practices. When used appropriately, presence is a priceless gift shared between two people.

Presence to the advisor is what the smell of fresh bread is to the senses—you cannot resist its pull. Undeniably alluring, its mouth-watering scent wafts through the air, triggering a positive mood in those entranced by its delectable aroma. Notice how you feel the next time you walk into a bakery. Perhaps you experience an immediate sense of calm. Maybe you recall pleasant memories of bygone days that cause you to smile. Such is the unmistakable draw one has when they are fully present with others.

In a similar way, presence is the feeling you get when you are at a concert. The program, with its instruments, musicians, room, lighting, and time of year together create an atmosphere of wonder you never want to end. I think back on the afternoon my wife and I saw the Broadway musical "Beautiful" which captures the life and music of Carole King. The performances were engaging; the stories behind the songs so memorable. The cast was passionate; the orchestration—brilliant! We were enthralled by every movement and sound. Sadly, we realized the show was over before we were ready for it to end. Recall a conversation or event you wanted to continue, but distractions or pressing obligations prevented that from happening. Sit for a few moments in the comfortable cushion of those memories. Then, re-engage prospects and clients mindful of how powerful presence can be both in your life and the lives of those you serve.

Our clients bring to the relationship their own brand of presence. Some clients are emotionally flat and hard to read. Others live conspicuously between two extremes: guarded or totally uninhibited. The advisor's challenge is to decipher what is revealed in each encounter. The ultimate goal is to create an atmosphere whereby both parties are comfortable interacting. There are hosts of phrases to describe this sweet spot: *we click; she gets me; it feels natural; we work well together; we are in the zone.* Each expression signals a connection between two people. A recent encounter I had with a client beautifully illustrates this dynamic.

Not long ago, a surprising email popped on my screen asking if I could be free for lunch in an hour. I replied, "Hard to believe, but I am." My friend of fifteen years was a senior level executive at a respected company. That day, she simply needed a listening ear and chose me as a trusted sounding board. We met for lunch at 11:45 the same day and spent quality time catching up on each other's lives.

During the conversation, she pulled a piece of paper from her purse. My friend read to me a well-written resignation letter that disclosed her resolve to retire her position after more than three decades in her industry. A milestone birthday was on the horizon and the time had come, at last, for her to move into the next phase of her life. What was not in the letter was an ongoing struggle she had with the company CEO. Although there were assurances made many times to relinquish leadership to a younger generation, the CEO of this closely-held company refused to let go. In good conscience, she could not continue in her role given these circumstances.

After asking a couple of questions, I said, "You have no idea how proud I am of you. Your personal courage and strength of character have never been as strong as now. Thank you for sharing this letter. Doing so pays me the highest compliment." I walked around our corner of the world for the next month shielding a story in my soul that soon would be public knowledge. Unexpected moments like this bear witness to the magic of two people attuned to one another. Clients who believe in us, who consider us an impenetrable fortress that protects a confidence, convey to us a high honor. Advisors who tap into the power of presence, who integrate the insights of stored memory build stronger connections.

Imagine your life for a moment as a wired circuit board that connects the mind with emotions, will, choices, and actions. Being in the zone with another person is when parts of our lives are talking in agreement. The emotions are firing messages to the brain that evoke a stamp of approval. The mind then sends a message to the will, conveying permission to give the self fully to the other person. The choice then toggles the "on" switch, determining the action that allows both individuals to bond. When we impart presence to another, our psyche endorses the moment and the individual. What happens next is predictable: you want to be with the other person and s/he wants to be with you.

Language used well, focused listening, learning about human behavior, emotions, and loss contribute to your presence quotient. Some would argue that only select people have "it" while others don't. I disagree. While every advisor's personality is unique, all of us can engage aspects of our interpersonal circuit board if we hope to transform our practice. Presence, therefore, is a necessary component in every successful social or business encounter. Without it, even the savviest advisor will miss opportunities to establish greater rapport with clients.

For all the good presence brings to a relationship, there is a downside called transference. Therapists will spend many hours developing a bond that facilitates healing and acceptance. Over time, a patient's feelings for a parent, lover, or partner may be transferred to the therapist, or "downloaded", often with sexual tension. Many have lost their licenses and have been defendants in malpractice proceedings because senseless improprieties polluted the patient-therapist relationship. In a similar way, advisors must stay in role, aware that the power of presence, when undisciplined, can take the advisor-client relationship in unhealthy directions. Rather than giving off mixed signals, remain aware of this subtle dynamic that can infiltrate the most professional of relationships.

Let us now explore the connectivity of interpersonal relationships using what I call the four "C's" of presence. Each of these is a formidable partner. Together they collaborate with the personality to form the person others perceive you to be.

Countenance

Like a delicate coping saw in the hands of a master carpenter, countenance is one of several characteristics that shape a relationship so it fits and feels right. It is the mental photograph someone takes of us or we take of ourselves—right or wrong. When we run low on energy or fail to look in the mirror before we head to the office, our mind prints that day's photo with muted colors. On the other hand, when we awaken rested and enthused, our inner snapshot of ourselves is textured with light and joy, communicating to others promising possibilities for the day ahead. This fair-weather interpretation of self is often how others see you, so go ahead— express yourself with a smile!

What is it about a smile that instantly draws one person to another? How often have you been moved from a dark place simply because someone smiled at you? Why does this generic facial expression so affect one's mood? From infancy, our parents' smiles said, "I'm crazy about you." During adolescence, we express our displeasure with a frown and our pleasure with a smile. As adults, we engage in activities and relationships that often elicit a smile. I believe everyone wants to be acknowledged, to have another say, "I like you!" A smile says all of that and more.

I have never understood why some find the gift of a smile uncomfortable to give and receive. If that is you, make a conscious effort today to showcase who you are. Look at your reflection in the mirror. Think of your happiest time. Take an imaginary photo and say, "Cheese!" Practice spreading your lips, turning the corners of your mouth upward and outward. As you begin your day, smile when you say "Good morning." Smile when you ask "How are you?" Smile as you answer the phone. Smile during the conversation. Putting the smile first, you smile others into smiling at you. It's magic!

Countenance also affects body language. A relaxed face and posture says, "I am at home in the body I have." This has been particularly difficult for me. Because I live with the aftershocks of polio, I walk with a pronounced limp. My left leg is almost an inch shorter than my right, thinner and lacking muscle tone. My gait is uniquely mine and I've grown to accept it. For 40 years, orthopedic surgeons have forecast that I'm several back and hip surgeries waiting to happen. So when I say, "Have a relaxed way with your body that communicates you are comfortable in your own skin," I tell myself to do the same.

Adults learn to sense when someone is not at ease with himself. In Chapter 6, we touched on nervousness as an emotion with which many people seem to live. Being ill-at-ease with who you are is a threat to being fully present to others. I remind you, even as I remind myself, that the body we have, whether in great shape, out-of-shape, or no shape is the only package we have to present ourselves to others. If I can limp my way through life for over 60 years and admit I look somewhat goofy as I walk along, you can face whatever it is that keeps you from feeling good about who you are. Sculpt a smile belonging to you and see its effect.

This feeling of pride in yourself goes beyond attitude. Physical, emotional and spiritual health are factors in countenance. Today's obesity crisis is at the forefront of a long list of ills that plague our society. I fight daily the battle of the bulge, yet I face this issue by viewing food as fuel. Published research confirms that the American diet is high in calories but low in nutrition. Do not rob yourself of feeling your best. Eat a diet rich in fresh vegetables, fruits, and lean protein. Take up some form of exercise. Your mind, body and spirit will thank you. Do I have my indulgences? Absolutely! I am hardly a fitness and nutrition poster child. I do know, however, I feel my best when I eat right, exercise, get adequate rest, and find time to be spiritually centered. These incremental, yet beneficial disciplines greatly contribute to a healthy image.

Finally, a robust countenance comes across in natural, non-threatening gestures. Our culture, so bombarded with sexualized images and messages, has made us terrified to give or receive a genuine, loving touch. Most employees nowadays take sensitivity training to become aware of how inappropriate language and touch can convey the wrong message. Sexual harassment is an ominous threat to human interactions in the workplace and other environments. One's professional bearing requires an awareness of how others perceive and receive any physical or verbal expression, no matter how harmless it may appear.

On the practical side of this issue, a warm, firm handshake with a client is not only needed but expected. Sometimes you may feel that a soft pat on the upper arm of a client is the right gesture to communicate your care. Many times I have been the initiator and recipient of a client hug. In almost every case, I ask, "May I give you a hug?" Friends and colleagues have never refused my outward expression of concern when their lives were not in a good place.

Conviction

Countenance is being comfortable in one's skin. Conviction, on the other hand, is strength in purpose and moral excellence in one's conduct. Like presence, it's mystery is unlocked with the key of awareness. It is sentient. You know when someone has "it." Conviction signals an anchoring message to clients who look to us for support, guidance, and service. They trust that no matter how stormy the sea, you, the advisor, have a sound inner core that will weather the elements and navigate them to a safe harbor.

But how does one find that support when the person needing a lift is you? The answer is nearby. Be alert to those moments when you are tempted to drag yourself to work looking for a pep talk. Every colleague, occupation, and career has challenges. There is no perfect work environment or ideal business situation. In the financial services business, compliance alone can at times strike fear in the hearts of all who have a Series 7 securities license. Sometimes an associate might be in the doldrums and require a bit more TLC. Other days you might be melancholy or affected by the pressures of life. We all have our moments when we are not exhibiting our best selves. The challenge is to limit the down times, accelerate the up times and learn to live in the balance.

Gary Player, the storied South African golfer, likes to tell audiences that when he gets up in the morning, he looks in the mirror and says, "Gary, today you can be happy or you can be miserable. Choose happy!" Conviction born in the womb of the will births an attitude about who we are that has the ability to transcend the passing ups and downs of a day. And yet, when it comes to work satisfaction, some advisors—perhaps even you—feel as if their legs are concrete columns and their feet shod with lead. When such a descent into professional sloth goes unchecked or unchanged, often there is little a trusted colleague can do. Peers who are in the grip of pessimism need a level of care not everyone can administer, but offer you must.

I was sharing lunch with a seminarian some 35 years ago when I sensed a level of despondency and pain I had not witnessed in him before. "Mark, you don't seem yourself today. What's going on?"

He looked away for a moment, gazed over the top of his tuna fish sandwich and said, "Tim, I don't know if I'm cut out to be a minister."

I looked into his sad eyes and asked, "Is it something at home, your family, a class we're taking, or your health?"

"Tim, a few families in the church are making my work so difficult, I don't know what to do."

We both were serving small churches that, for decades, had called seminary students to be their pastors. Both churches were similar in size, about 50 miles from Louisville, Kentucky, but in opposite directions.

Fishing for a reaction, I asked, "Don't you love the ministry?"

Without missing a beat, he said, "I love the ministry, Tim. It's people I can't stand!"

All of us have times in our professional lives when we feel exactly like Mark. We enjoy the work we do: solving problems, helping individuals better their lives, offering our best counsel in the face of difficulties. But there are moments—even seasons—when our conviction runs low and our spirit flags to the point of exhaustion. When it happens, take a few days off. Do something that restores your strength and reconnects you with the core convictions that led you into your profession.

My present source of renewal is reading. Though my education required me to pour over thousands of volumes and articles, it was only after I finished graduate school that I learned to read for enjoyment. Years ago a good friend asked me, "Tim, do you ever read anything for fun?"

I looked down and said, "No, not really."

He placed a somewhat cheesy Louis L'Amour yarn in my hand. "Read this book and get lost in the story. It'll do you good."

Well, it did me better than good. That experience began a habit I continue to this day. Whether it's reading a novel, canoeing a placid lake, walking through a quiet city park, or playing kickball with your children, develop energizing habits that reconnect you to basic convictions about who you are, what you do, and why you do it. Rediscover the power of presence, perhaps for the first time, reflectively in your own soul. Notice life taking on a different hue.

Fundamentally, presence feeds on professional conviction. We all have experienced a dynamic speaker who commands attention without trying, whose very presence makes you stand taller, who emotes with such resolve, "I believe I am making a difference because of the work I have chosen to do!" When you meet such a person, you are witnessing someone who, at her core, is living at peak levels. I am thinking of an individual in the investment business who is also in senior management with the firm for which I work. Every time I have heard him speak, I have marveled at his level of energy, the passion with which he communicates the message, and the magnetic pull of his personality. When you hear someone like that, you stand a bit straighter, summoned by words anchored to beliefs that are by definition transformational. Such passion for and in your work will connect you with more clients, attract more prospects, and extinguish doubts about the validity of your calling. Be convicted in all you do communicating a presence that draws others to you.

Confidence

Confidence is a belief in yourself and your abilities. It is a strong, winsome personality; not swagger or egotism. This self-assuredness is an awareness that you have something to offer that no one else can give. Likewise, it is not a put down of others as much as it is a "lift up" of your own abilities, gifts, and interests. Not to be confused with cockiness or over-assertiveness, confidence is neither "overly" anything nor focused on self. When someone has an infectious personality, you intuitively know that confidence is alive and well in that person.

Artists who perform as soloists know the power of confidence. A celebrated pianist, prima donna, principal dancer or diva cannot command world audiences without it. When an artist has stage presence, the evening is nothing less than magic, mystery—celebration! Without it, the critics howl, the crowds dwindle, the invitations stop. In a like manner, an authentic sense-of-self courses through the veins of corporate leaders who understand the relationship between growing a business and caring for those working in the trenches. And yes, advisors who have confidence hear trumpets calling them to work day after day because they know they are making a difference in someone's life.

I have heard Don Connelly share a story that says it all. When you board an airliner, find your seat, buckle your seatbelt, and hear the cabin door close, what kind of voice do you want to hear from the cockpit? "Ladies and gentlemen, welcome to flight 564 from Atlanta to Los Angeles. This is Captain George Uncertain with First Officer Sheila Terrified, based in Maybe, Missouri." Now keep listening. "Our flight plan today is, hopefully, to take off in the next hour, climbing through what could be rough air to a cruising altitude of, let's say 30,000 feet. Now sit back, try to relax, and know that even though this is our first flight in this plane, we are going to do everything we can, using all the skill we know, to get you to LA safely and on time." Hearing that, you unbuckle, get up, grab your carry-on, and demand to get off the plane!

When you fly, you expect a pilot who speaks with certainty. His voice tells you all is well. Such a professional enjoys being a pilot because it is the work he loves to do. Hearing a confident voice over the plane's intercom, you sit back, relax, and know you will arrive at your destination on time and safely. There is no substitute for professional confidence. Without it, you convey a weakness that creates doubt and fear.

This aplomb grows as we constantly learn how best to work with clients: enjoying their friendship, utilizing resources, implementing ideas, suggesting strategies. There will be times when confidence fails. Other times it will be called into question. No one can serve every client with absolute perfection in every possible situation. The markets will go against a trade. A recession will turn the investment world in the direction of a den teeming with bears. You will misunderstand a client's needs or make an honest mistake when you recommend he go in one direction rather than another. Detours show up, the weather changes, and life can throw more than a few curve balls just when the game is on the line. Go about your business with an assuredness that you know more about creating and managing an investment strategy than any client you serve. It flexes a muscle that signals to clients you can get them to their destination safely and on time.

The professional who has pitched her tent with clients and their families believes that no matter what shows up, they can handle it. Such presence not only draws clients and prospects to us; it allows them to invite others who need the gifts we have to give.

Compassion

Countenance, conviction, and confidence, vital as they are, hold no quarter with compassion. This transforming reality is the catalyst that changes a warm body from simply "showing up" to "being fully present." Countenance without compassion is acting. Conviction without compassion is egotism. Confidence without compassion is self-promotion. But compassion, woven into the fabric of countenance, conviction, and confidence creates a transformational presence unlike any other. Compassion changes the way an advisor engages a client, allowing empathy and sympathy a greater seat of influence during each engagement.

Compassion at some level is welded into the structure of the human spirit. Some of us have limitless wells of care from which to draw the water of comfort and understanding without end. For others, compassion seems to lie dormant, undisturbed, almost untouched by human brokenness. Mental health professionals quickly raise a hand to say that each person's ability to exhibit compassion goes back to imprinting experiences from infancy. We know that babies not cuddled and touched frequently tend to arrive at adulthood with crippling emotional deficits. You will serve clients who were shortchanged in their early years. Hugs were infrequent or absent. Verbal and physical demonstrations of compassion and love were rare. Just know, expressions of genuine care to adults with such a past may be met at arm's length.

What is at stake here? The word compassion is the merging of the preposition *com* meaning "with" and *passion* meaning "feeling." To express compassion is to *feel with* another some pain, joy, life-view, struggle, disappointment, or perspective. Being a compassionate advisor goes beyond being there for your client when an unexpected tragedy strikes. We can get stuck on that one idea of compassion because it is shown by others primarily in the broken moments of life. But compassion covers as wide a spectrum of human connection as the rainbow's reach from infrared to ultraviolet. And because presence and compassion are so integral to each other, the caring advisor will call on their gifts frequently.

For example, look at a client and the difficulty he feels preparing for retirement. Confident in your ability, embracing conviction in your calling, you *feel with* this client his struggle. I am having this very conversation with many clients right now. When I hear a man or woman say, "I'm not sure I can walk away from a job I have loved for 35 years," I allow those words to express my personal struggle with that very issue. For just a few minutes, I put myself in their place. I see the future through their eyes and bear the sense of impending loss they are feeling. It was Plato who advised, "Be kind, for everyone you meet is fighting a harder battle."

A client might sit with you in your office elated over her daughter's upcoming marriage. Perhaps, as a married adult, you can listen and *feel with* this mother the joy in seeing her daughter marry a wonderful man. You also share in her anxiety about a relationship that is sure to change. Compassion is always on alert when we are present to others. We sense what they sense, we listen to hear what they hear; we open our eyes, mind and heart to feel what they feel and see what they see, all in the good work of being a caring presence to and with them.

The focused listening partner we met called intuition is a powerful ally with compassion. A client recently told me his number associated with retirement. No, it wasn't the money he needs to retire; it was the number of years before he plans to walk away from what he has done for the last 30 years. He said, almost in passing, "I plan to do this another five or six years and then do something else."

Knowing him well, I responded, "I may have a similar number, but I'm not sure how I feel about traditional retirement."

He quickly intuited what I might say. "I'm with you, Tim. I can't imagine not waking up doing something productive as long as my health allows."

In a totally unscripted exchange, I found myself feeling with my client. He put the words out there, hanging between us for a few seconds; happening instantaneously, emotionally impactful. Compassion was not some overwhelming feeling of care as both of us sat identifying with each other. Rather, it was an instantaneous connection as our stories briefly merged. My hunch is that many of us have similar moments more often than we may realize.

Then, of course, there are those life-altering events in your client's life when you must summon a level of compassion you did not know you possessed. You attend the funeral for a woman whose husband has been both client and friend. You sit through the memorial service and remember the times when the three of you were "in the zone" planning retirement, dreaming about grandchildren, facing the loss of parents, celebrating the last payment on a dream home you helped them finance. You sit there, with memory as your friend, tears trickling down your cheeks as you ask yourself, "How will I be present to Bill now that the love of his life is gone?" A few days later, you call him to check-in and invite him to breakfast or coffee. You tell yourself there will be no business talk when you get together. No, you will have a much more important agenda: simply being a presence to this man who has no idea how he will go on without his soulmate.

In the regular cadence of a practice, these four C's fuse, becoming allies in our work, creating an atmosphere that changes having clients into transformational experiences with men and women. Imagine yourself being that nurturing presence in the lives of others. Honor the gifts you alone have to share. When you do, they will change you and the people you serve.

LOOKING BACK

■   Presence with clients is the canvas on which we practice the advisory craft. Full presence requires integration of the four C's.

■   Countenance is the aura or presentation the clients see when they look in your face, glimpse the energy in your eyes, see the smile on your face, and experience the person you are.

■   Conviction is an absolute belief that the work you do with clients makes a difference in their lives.

■   Confidence acts on the talents, training, and skills you have as a credentialed financial or life advisor. It is not self-promotion.

■   Compassion enables us to "feel with" another.

NOW WHAT?

1. Jot down the names of two people you know who exude a healthy presence.

What qualities do they have in common? How might you distinguish what may be personality from a skill you could employ in your life?

Constantly observe, question, and ask how your life and practice could be better if you would _____. Dismiss from your mind that some people "have it" but others don't.

2. How do you embrace your role as an advisor? In what ways do your personal convictions and professional confidence shape your practice?

Akin to our discussion of authority in Chapter 4, conviction and confidence are servants to professionals who wear the advisor mantle. When we are at ease in our role, prospects and clients are drawn to us.

3. Who is the most compassionate person you know in your unique business environment? Are you comfortable sympathizing or conveying concern? If not, can you name the origin of that discomfort?

At compassion's core is the ability to see the perspective or feel the emotion of another person. Learn to recognize those moments. Even in brief exchanges with others, note how it knits your lives together. Apply that feeling in your work with clients and notice how relationships transform.

Chapter 9

Facing Limitations

To all the activities I have wanted to do across these last six decades—skating, skiing, running—my body's physical limitations have shouted, "No way!" The after-effects of the polio virus have been a constant and at times unforgiving teacher, reminding me that while the heart is willing, the flesh will not cooperate. Even still, I have learned the sky is not the limit when reaching for personal and professional success. To face our limitations is not to be defined by them. They can, with discipline, become some of our strangest, strongest allies.

Early on, my parents encouraged me to test my physical abilities, knowing I would discover my own limitations in life's crucible of experiences. Of all the enduring gifts they gave me—a loving home, faith, an inquisitive mind, courage—music and the ability to play the piano still energizes my life. Even there, sitting at the keyboard, I know my limitations while celebrating the pianistic prowess of virtuosos who play at the highest level.

Limitations. We all have them. Some, like my withered left leg and limp, are obvious. Many learn to mask their flaws while others fear ever admitting to them. And yet, to those who dare travel down the road of discovery, whole worlds of opportunity await. Being aware of our limitations can enhance the work we do and inspire the people that make our work possible. It is my thesis that limitation awareness separates advisors who know their clients' stories well from the herd of advisors who choose only to work on the investment side of the relationship. In what follows, we consider three dimensions of our work where we face limitations: those we face professionally, ones we meet in clients, and those inescapable issues we see in ourselves.

Professional Limitations

The financial services industry, following the 2009 market meltdown, has become one of the most regulated segments of our economy. The number of bank and market regulations that include Dodd-Frank and all its children, coupled with the public's demand for greater oversight of the industry, has challenged every financial firm and all advisors. Whether you work for a storied Wall Street firm, a bank, or are an independent, the number of regulations continues to grow at a record pace. The question hangs in the air: how does any advisor maintain the confidence needed to guide clients towards their goals without second-guessing almost every syllable of advice?

The CERTIFIED FINANCIAL PLANNER™ designation I hold requires 30 hours of continuing education every two years. The firm where I work has regular, appropriate continuing education modules required by either my federal securities license or firm management. These CE courses guide us to know firm policy and the public's need for ethical, professional, and competent services. Such ongoing education brings with it a reminder that we work within the limitations established by the law and market regulators. These limitations protect the public from predators who poach for the vulnerable in addition to erecting a structure the majority of professional advisors need and want. So where does that leave the advisor when working with clients?

First, everyone needs to know that none of us in the business can do whatever we please when it comes to managing money. By investing in our clients' stories, including their limitations, advisors can reveal and discuss the confines imposed on them as they do their work. All of us have had conversations with a prospect who believes our days are spent buying and selling stocks like nineteenth-century auctioneers sold tobacco. I hasten to say that some in the business build their practice around clients who want high-volume trading, expecting high returns in exchange. Most advisors know that this is not only unwise but financially unsound. Clients, however, have to be cautioned. From time to time I tell clients, "Not only is that not a good idea, but it may be detrimental to you and your economic future."

The public also must be educated to understand we work in an industry bolstered with impenetrable fences that protect individual investors from the consequences of unchecked greed. I reassure clients throughout the year, "We deal with this situation in this way to protect you, our firm, and me." Why is this so important? One simple reason: clients need to know that the misuse or abuse of money has devastating consequences.

Second, the industry limits how we can help our clients. We have learned already that involved advisors invest extra time, energy, and curiosity into every client encounter. Those very investments create vast amounts of information that call on compassion in times of client distress. The business, however, prohibits us from lending a client money or co-signing a bank note to help them through a tough time. We are told "No" to paying for gifts or entertainment above specified limits or any other imagined ways to help a client—all for good reason! Our industry reminds us there are appropriate and inappropriate ways to be supportive. We cannot become enablers of client behavior that is destructive for the client and for those with whom they share life. The business has said there are limitations on the assistance we can offer clients. When we remind ourselves where those boundaries lie, we strengthen our ability to be even more transparent than when we tip-toe around the rules. Yes, there are times when, like you, I would burn all the regulations and naively imagine everyone with "Financial Advisor" printed on a business card to be ethical. History reminds us such is not the case. Even with the high moral standards I have set for myself staring me in the face, I am still human. I know that any random day, I am capable of acting in ways that are not indicative of my best self. Professional limitations are a friend—sometimes a troubling friend, but a friend nonetheless.

Client Limitations

Finding client assets is at the heart of the financial planning process. The discovery of assets is time-consuming, but not difficult. We ask questions about where cash is held, where other assets are invested; if the client is participating in a 401(k) plan and whether the company has a defined benefit or pension plan. We probe deeper to find if they have traditional, Roth, or inherited IRAs. As part of this exploration, we discover whether the client has life or long-term care insurance, disability, or a buy-sell agreement that uses life insurance. Does the client own a business or real estate? If so, is the property mortgaged or do they own it outright? On and on go the financial questions from the beginning of the relationship through times of review and life-change. We cannot effectively accomplish the planning task without knowing all the financial details of our clients' lives.

More important than uncovering the difficult, hard-to-get-at information about your clients' assets and liabilities is knowing their limitations. We can reduce to numbers and models the financial data. Discovering client limitations, however, is as important as knowing where the money is. All clients have limitations; some more, some less, all impacting whether or not you and they will realize success in the advisor-client relationship. Suppose you acquire clients with the following financial profile:

■   A couple married 39 years.
■   Husband 64, working; wife 63, retired school teacher; both in good health.
■   two children; five grandchildren.
■   Investible assets of $1.6 million ($1 million qualified; $600,000 taxable).

■   A home fully owned valued at $675,000.
■   Four rental properties appraised at $530,000 with $268,000 mortgaged.
■   No long-term care or life insurance.

The couple seems compatible. They are quite comfortable talking about their financial life and the planning process. The husband tells you he plans to work another five years but the wife protests, hoping he retires at Social Security's full retirement age, which for him is 66. As you probe further into their family life, their children's careers, the love of their grandchildren, you touch a nerve when you ask, "Can you tell me about parents who are still living?" Suddenly...quiet. He looks at her, she looks at him, and says, "Do you want to talk about your mother or should I?" How do you react? What do you say? When you look up—poof!—the elephant in the room appears. Be the leader; break the silence.

"I can see this is a difficult topic but I need to know what's going on between the two of you regarding your mother."

The wife begins to cry. The husband, also teary-eyed says, "I'll share her story."

You, the advisor, listen, focus, and learn. Now staring them in the face, beyond an impeccable balance sheet of acquired assets, is a parent with a chronic health issue possibly living another 15 years. You learn the couple bears a shared responsibility to care for the wife's mother with her brother and sister who each lives more than 1,000 miles away. On top of the health concern, the mother is resisting a change in her living situation from a home with a yard, maintenance, and upkeep to an assisted living facility nearby. This couple, five years from a wonderful season of life they have imagined for decades, is now dealing with a limitation they cannot ignore.

Imagine another retirement-aged couple with a similar financial profile who look at you with an air of despondency when you ask, "Is there someone in your family for whom you are responsible?" You learn the wife, 63, is recently retired. However, the husband,

64, hoping to retire in five years, has a 61-year-old special needs brother who lives with them who may need an increased level of care in the years ahead. This family is facing a limitation of another kind, nonetheless present and equally impactful. If your practice is anything like ours, you will discover in almost every family some kind of limitation that must be identified and addressed with sensitivity.

Health challenges present another tranche of limitations, becoming potentially debilitating as we age. In our practice, we have husbands caring for wives crippled by Alzheimer's. We have more than a few wives caring for their husbands, often at home, with no children living nearby to offer support. Widows and widowers who continue to live by themselves face loneliness and no small measure of fear. That fear—of being incapacitated, unable to call for help, feeling unsafe—limits the client's perspective on everything from lowering risk in a portfolio to knowing when to take a required distribution from an IRA.

Health-related restraints are a reminder to advisors to revisit the document topic with clients. Is their estate plan in need of a professional review? Have they updated their medical advance directives and financial powers? Will they share with us their children's contact information? How do they feel about sharing their financial situation with their children? If they approve disclosure, do we have a letter of authorization on file? If they have long term care insurance, are either eligible for benefits? Almost every place we look has an impact on the way we engage clients affected by declining health.

Caring advisors will also have their antennae up when discovering a client owns a business. A few years ago, a new client of mine came to an impasse with his long-time business partner. Business partnerships can, over time, become imbalanced when it comes to the non-financial investment needed to sustain the enterprise. In this situation, my client was shouldering 90% of the sales and management responsibilities while his partner leisurely drifted in and out of the business pursuing non-profit, volunteer opportunities. As you might imagine, he was expecting the same compensation, share of profits, and equal say in how the business operated. My client offered to buy him out, trying a number of unsuccessful tactics. Ultimately, these partners embarked on a 6-year litigation. My client eventually filed for bankruptcy. When both parties laid down their weapons, the business was insolvent. In the end, the only winners were the lawyers.

Knowing all about a client's business is imperative if we are to bring to the table our full expertise. If the client does not have a lock-tight "buy-sell" agreement, succession plan in place, adequate liability insurance coverage, not to mention a 401(k) or SEP-IRA, decisions made at the personal level will suffer. Is it an equal partnership? Are there multiple business partners? Are children involved as employees or stockholders? Is the business viable or is it in a volatile market? Ask questions about the business structure for the sole purpose of being resource-ready.

The fourth area of human limitations is mental health. Clients with personal or family emotional and psychological issues are, most of the time, reluctant to discuss them because of the embarrassment associated with mental illness in our society. We all bear a level of shame for not being more sensitive and educated about this malaise and its pervasive effects. When someone is taking medication for any number of maladies, we react almost with pride when we share that we too are taking a similar med. But when we learn a person struggles with manic-depressive illness, schizophrenia, or some form of psychosis, we may not only turn the other way, but label them with objectionable terms.

Advisors must find a way to learn about the mental health of clients and persons for whom they are responsible. How do you broach such a conversation? Imagine sitting with a couple, both in their early 60s, planning to retire in several years. First, ask a question that will open the door for further exploration. Ask them if there is mental illness in their families. Justify your question with examples of other clients in your practice who, for example, struggle with depression as you sensitively discussed financial matters. Listen with compassion as displayed in your body language. Extend a hand, move closer, offer a hug. Be fully present and offer hope.

What you do not want to happen in the client-advisor relationship is to be rocking along for years when you call the husband to discuss a planning matter, only to learn from the wife that he has been hospitalized. As she explains, you learn for the first time that your client battles depression, has been under psychiatric care, and now his medications are no longer effective. Caring for clients through a season of decline brings to the surface of our own lives those power partners of compassion, empathy, and service that other advisors may possess, but have ignored by being only focused on the investment side of the relationship.

Other personal limitations not explored here would include a laundry basket of issues like clients who live great distances from aging parents, adult children, grandchildren; financial problems that prevent clients from pursuing retirement dreams; faith crises...the list goes on. In every case, when discovering client limitations, ask sensitive questions, respond compassionately, and then jointly, discuss options to guide the client towards his goals.

I have a model of a sailboat on my desk at home that was given to me by a close friend. Printed on the mainsail are these words attributed to Bertha Calloway: "We cannot direct the wind, but we can adjust our sails." Knowing where our clients face personal limitations will not change how the wind blows, but it will empower us to adjust our sails to do our very best work for those who look to us for support.

Advisor Limitations

Personal limitations in our lives as advisors may be the most difficult to define. When it comes to the business, we can read the regulations, follow the rules, and bend to the requests of compliance officers when they call. When it comes to our clients, we see with uncommon clarity what they dare to reveal: glaring dysfunctional family dynamics, health crises, business and emotional challenges and more. But when it comes to ourselves, it is difficult to take that piercing, revelatory stare in the mirror. Limitations dim the bright light of an overly confident ego, clouded by the trials we help others face. In no greater area of our work does self-awareness and candor demand our attention.

From my own life engagement with the residual fallout from polio, I come to this subject from a uniquely personal point of view. You may not agree with or see the world from where I sit, but for good or ill, this approach has helped me cope with a physical deficit for more than 60 years. Several decades ago, I came face to face with the fact that no matter what orthotic device was placed on my left foot or attached to my left leg, I would never walk without a limp—ever. This is the hand I was dealt. I could forever mourn the loss of normal mobility and facility or I could celebrate the abundant gifts in my life. I chose the champion's way; I chose acceptance. As I have said now for more than 25 years, "I have a limp, but the limp doesn't have me."

It is precisely from this place we begin our conversation. Though hard to do, all of us must find private, uninterrupted time to stare critically and subjectively into the mirror of our lives. This exercise is not that of Narcissus (from which we get the word "narcissism" or intense, ego-consumed self-love) but rather that of an honest, grateful, and very normal person. Such a sober look at ourselves is also not a "one and done" event. Some of our personal limitations, like my limp, stay with us forever. Others evolve as seasons change. We mature, health fails, children leave home, and so forth. Know this, everyone who walks planet earth has limitations we share with all humanity. Rather than being a sign of weakness, knowing our limitations frees us to be fully the self-aware, though limited person God created us to be.

Limitations are as varied as the chromosomes in our cells. Some are artistically short-changed while others exhibit genius. Many have athletic ability; few are MVP worthy. The personal defects with which some deal every day are painful: abusive childhoods, a failed marriage, business failures and career dead-ends, personality quirks, even how we deal with humor and our reaction to happenstance all involve limitations. We as advisors must bravely face our own before we can be effective in helping clients face theirs. Being honest about our own shortcomings is where we begin forming the foundation on which we learn to deal with the limps we have rather than the limps dealing with us.

Write down the list of limitations you share with everyone and those you see only in yourself. Remember, this exercise is not a group project. Be honest, self-critical, self-aware, transparent, leaving nothing off the list that would be an accurate reflection of where you sense you come up short. Write the first words that come to your mind; they are often the best words.

This rigorous personal inventory is not unlike one of the steps in Alcoholics Anonymous "12-Step Program," where you have a list, written down on a slip of paper, naming your own unique personal limitations. Circle all you share with the world at large and then list them again in a column by themselves. Look at the words that remain. Rewrite them on a column adjacent to those limitations we all share. As you rewrite your personal limitations, say each word aloud. Why? Every mental health professional I know reminds me that hearing the sound of our own voice is a powerful tool in etching into our minds the message we most need to hear. Coaches know this when they have the team cheer in unison, "We're Number One! We're Number One!" Motivational speakers will often have an audience repeat affirmations aloud: "I am a person of worth who has gifts to share," or "If it's going to be, it's up to me!" These are two of many I have repeated when participating in a motivational seminar.

Now look at the two lists. Glance at the short list of limitations we all share and then look at the longer list that is uniquely yours. Is there one or two that say the same thing? Does another come to mind that you could to add to the list? If so, add it. When you have finished this part of the exercise, get an envelope, place your list in the envelope and seal it. On the outside of the envelope write the date two days from the time you seal it. Now place that envelope where you will see it and walk away.

Two days later, find 30 minutes of private time to open the envelope and revisit what you have written. Like the first time, look at the short list on the left of those shared human limitations and then speak out the longer list of your personal limitations on the right. Turn the page over and write at the top this question: "What gifts do I have to give others having now discovered my own personal limitations?" Begin writing down those discoveries one after the other. Don't become distracted by a side thought or the temptation to analyze your list. Simply write down what first comes to your mind without stopping.

You will see and hear the names of those personal fences you have erected around yourself. You will also smile in revisiting the gifts you have to offer to those on your path. You may not accomplish everything you might hope to achieve. I believe Mozart died with symphonies unwritten in his soul. Every life is in some way an incomplete sentence. What you will learn through this simple, self-directed exercise is an appreciation of who you are, bound by your limitations, and what you alone can bring to others who look to you for support, community, professional guidance, and friendship.

This self-inventory is an exercise I would recommend you do at least annually. The demands of business, the responsibilities to spouses, children, friends, and community can weigh heavily on us. Once we feel that pressure, we slump into emotional exhaustion because we have forgotten who we are. We lose sight of what we cannot be, are not gifted to be, and maybe even what we refuse to be because of our values. We live, move and operate in our business and personal lives within confines, yet we simultaneously choose to celebrate the gifts we have and must give. Live and work out of that sense of giftedness even though bound by limitations. When you do, you will become even more the consummate professional you want to be in this good work.

LOOKING BACK

■   Every business, organization, individual, and family has limitations.

■   Some limitations we share with everyone; others belong to a smaller population. Even fewer belong uniquely to us.

■   Every person has gifts to share. When we name and embrace our limitations, we begin to see those gifts with greater clarity and we do our best work.

■   Find ways to affirm and incorporate your clients' gifts into your practice while helping them see and accept their limitations.

Chapter 10

Check In

We now meander into an aspect of practice management that some do instinctively while others only reluctantly or fail to do altogether. To "check in" is to touch base with three dimensions of practice that affect the work we do. In the following pages, we will explore how we check in with clients, how we check in with our role, but most importantly, how we check in with ourselves and significant others who love and support us. Weaving this behavior into the tapestry of our practice creates an environment of mutual care that changes an ordinary financial services business into a transforming interpersonal experience.

CLIENTS

Being intentional about client reviews is central to the work of a financial advisor. We revisit planning conversations and investment goals, remember information shared about the client's job, family, or health, and evaluate portfolio performance in light of the overall market. Scheduling, preparing and conducting those meetings—whether in the office or over the phone—takes time but is an integral part of the business.

It is those moments in-between reviews where advisors can easily (and dare I say unknowingly) drop the ball. Checking in with clients several times a year to hear their voice and for them to hear ours communicates a level of care that more than a few advisors miss. Clients, however, remember those calls and, at least in my experience, will bring them to mind when least expected.

Keeping in touch is an art; a gestured reaching out that assures the client, "You are not alone." A second thought is conveyed to them that may be even more comforting: "I genuinely care about you."

Let us look at a few reasons why I recommend you check in with clients between those expected reviews. Though not exhaustive, this list of seven client touch points will quicken your imagination to think of additional reasons why checking in can transform that relationship.

Loneliness

More of our clients live alone than we may realize. Like you, I immediately think of the recently widowed or divorced. Those who have never married or adults who have lost what was at one time a committed partner feel a vacuous pain created by the absence of someone whom they loved. A single woman sat in my office not too long ago and remarked to me that the loneliness she knows has lasted close to 30 years. Surrounded by work colleagues and close friends, she opens the door to an empty house night after night asking why life, at least for her, has been so solitary. Widowers may have greater difficulty than widows dealing with loneliness. Men tend to isolate themselves, often not knowing how to be vulnerable and transparent even to friends they have known for decades. That is not to say that women do not experience a unique set of challenges. In my pastoral work and now as an advisor, I have witnessed this difference between the sexes that may have more to it than what can be casually observed.

Feelings that impinge on societal issues, moral concerns, ethical ambiguities and spiritual struggles can exacerbate deep loneliness. This void is more than believing others do not understand us; it goes to the heart of what it means to wrestle with a life that serves up more questions than answers, leaving us twisting in the fierce wind of helplessness. We do good work when we check in with men and women in our practice who we believe may be going through a season of loneliness. "How are you doing? You've been on my mind recently and I simply wanted to call to see how you were." Those two sentences will not remove loneliness from another life, but they communicate a care that is integral to who we are and the profession we have chosen.

Values Conflict

If we are in touch with those moments when words are exchanged, we may pick up a conflict in values gnawing at a client's conscience. Such a conflict could show up at the door of an investment the client holds. Owning or considering the purchase of defense, gaming, alcohol, and even energy stocks can raise values questions that demand a hearing. A person's sense of morality and ethics is a deeply personal, often mysterious resident in the human soul. How we feel about shared values forms bonds with some and erects barriers with others.

When we call a client and bring up a previous conversation about values, we communicate a sensitivity to feelings that can be easily overlooked. Checking in with a client struggling with values-related questions regarding certain holdings might be as simple as forwarding to her an article on socially responsible investing. You may be associated with a firm that has access to money managers who specialize in this investment niche. If you have clients with specific religious concerns, you will want to ask them if there are areas of investment best avoided. A conflict in values acknowledged by an advisor gives the client more reasons to listen to your counsel and warm to your friendship. Check in when you sense this type of conflict. You will discover a client grateful for and even surprised by your concern.

Family Stress

Family stressors may be the most important of these seven dimensions of care. They cry out for our attention. A client may have shared with you that an aging parent is moving to an assisted-living facility or now needs around the clock home care. Parents who have sacrificed to educate their children may have a son or daughter, diploma in hand, with no job or job prospects on the horizon. A fire may have damaged a significant part of a client's home or burned it to the ground. You offered support and helped them find temporary housing. You also suggested a few options to handle the financial stress such a tragedy presents. But that was two months ago and the client, now more than ever, needs you to check in and ask how the family is coping.

A marriage of many years will face some level of stress when a spouse retires several years before the other spouse is able to do the same. Knowing that unique dynamic is a good reason to pick up the phone, call the working spouse, and ask if you can meet for lunch. The same gesture of support follows as you check in with the spouse who has retired. Three months later, you call to ask how days are being spent in this new season of life. Husbands and wives who find themselves as caregivers for their mates long for a friendly, caring voice on the other end of the phone even if the call lasts no more than a minute or two. That tenured aspect of family stress tends to take up permanent residence, longing for caring friends and professional partners to say, "I'm here for you."

Career Uncertainty

Work counselors tell us that most adults will change careers two, three, or more times during the course of their lives. At age 50, I re-invented my professional life, moving away from pastoral ministry to the work of being a financial advisor. During those transition months many years ago, the people I still remember "being there" found me on e-mail or reached me by phone. They checked in to see how I was doing and how our family was managing this change in my life. They weren't trying to be nosey; they simply wanted my wife and me to know that they cared and believed the best years of our lives were still before us.

Sitting with clients for a review is a perfect time to ask how their respective careers are going. When you learn of a longing to find another line of work, be the first to ask if they have a resume. If they do, ask them to share it with you and offer to keep your ear to the ground about possible work opportunities or career counseling services with which you may be aware. And then, a couple weeks later, check in with them. Remind them of the conversation about a career change and ask if they still feel the need to move in another direction. Listen, offer what help you deem appropriate, and then call again two weeks later. We spend a third or more of our lives at work. Clients who wrestle with career uncertainty, with help, discover a heightened sense of purpose that energizes their present and points them to a better future.

Goal Confusion

It is difficult if not impossible to know how to get to where you want to go if you do not first know where you are. If I want to get to San Francisco, I need to know that I am in Atlanta rather than Anchorage if I have any hope of arriving at my destination. Likewise, a client who presents goal confusion may be communicating a deep uncertainty about where they are at this moment in life. Asking clients about goals is a fertile field for conversation. Why? Because goals affect financial planning, investment choices, risk appetite, and cash flow. Goals that include world travel create a different set of demands than goals that focus on spending time with grandchildren across town.

Be mindful that asking about ambitions and getting answers requires us to write down those responses or etch them so deeply in our memories we associate them with a particular client. Between review meetings, check in about a goal and find out what progress is being made. You might notice an article that addresses that goal. Clip it out of the newspaper, send the link in an e-mail, and let the client know you were thinking of them when you read the article. Making the journey with clients may have you thinking more about your own life and where career, family, time, interests, and faith are taking you. That discovery—with clients and yourself—is potentially life-changing.

Event Triggers

An event trigger is anything that happens in a client's world that might affect her well-being. A flood devastates a neighborhood where three clients live. A fire spreads to rural acreage close to a farm owned by another. A tornado touches down in a community near the university a client's child attends. A measles outbreak closes down a school where several of your clients' grandchildren are students. You get the idea. Caring advisors find a way to check in with clients and their families when a catastrophic event occurs. Times are, we learn about a client challenge long after the event has passed. When that happens, call or e-mail asking about his or her well-being and that of the family. I have learned it's rarely too late to express care.

Health Challenges

The seventh, but no doubt the most important time to check in with clients is because of health challenges. Our practice has individuals who live with cancer, Alzheimer's, Parkinson's, partial or total blindness, stroke consequences, paralysis, mentally and physically challenged children, and mobility constraints. Adults whom I have known through the years facing these and other health challenges have confided to me that the greatest fear they have is being ignored or forgotten.

Good health allows adults to stay involved in their family, community, congregation, neighborhood, friendships, and profession. When health fails, connecting with others is often the casualty. Picking up the phone or writing a brief personal note of encouragement means more to the recipient than any of us who are healthy can imagine.

Checking in with clients in these seven areas is so important when we are intentional about this good work. Sad to say, but good intentions fall by the wayside when the demands of less personal work stare us in the face. Note these three simple steps you can take to incorporate checking in with clients into your daily routines:

■ Make a list of your clients whom you sense has one or more of these seven presenting life challenges.
■ Task yourself to check in with each of these clients.
■ Assign no more than three check-ins per, 12-15 per week. The purpose of the call or note is not to talk about business but simply to let them know you are thinking about them.

ROLE

Being a financial advisor is one of the most honorable professions anyone could have. In spite of the headlines airing the dirty laundry of a few in our business, the overwhelming majority of advisors are morally and ethically focused on doing the right thing in the right way at the right time with the right resources to serve those who look to us for advice.

Unfortunately, sometimes even the best among us lose their way in the demanding, at times lonely work placed in our hands. We take on ourselves the burden of a choppy or falling market and the returns that follow those declines. We second guess recommendations we have made and the wisdom of placing client assets in certain investments. If we share life with family, our spouse or partner can feel the effects of that stress in loss of affection or, at times, misplaced anger. Ours is a high and noble calling that brings with it immense personal and professional pressure.

Checking in as a financial advisor requires us to step away from the business on a regular basis. Such "time away" could be a few hours once a week, an afternoon a couple times a month, or a full day away to simply think about the balance between our personal and business lives. To fail at self-care is to forego sound physical and mental health, but ultimately, to fail at self-care is to betray those we serve.

Someone has rightly said that all of us have an address, but some of us are never home. Our body may be at our desk, our frame in the office, but our soul, the person we are is absent. We are either off in an imaginary, better place, or we are shut down inside unable to connect with who we are, unavailable to others who look to us for support. Any professional role that has leadership written into the job description demands an address. We have to be "there" to serve as an example to those we lead and to impart to them the importance of the work we do. A first place to check in with your role is to periodically move away from the work for the sole purpose of returning to the work with greater energy and focus.

It has been some two decades now since I received the gift of a sabbatical. The church I served offered me a month's leave in addition to my annual one-month vacation after serving the congregation five years. I chose as my venue Regent's Park College, Oxford University. There, over the course of three unscripted weeks, I completed a book manuscript that came to print later that year. During those three weeks, I attended various lectures, read, wrote, and at times slept. Though our work rarely affords us such a hiatus, find a way to schedule a couple days here or there every three or four months for one sole purpose: self-renewal and rest.

A second step is to check in with the realistic expectations that come with the territory. Highly motivated and driven men and women fall into what I call "fantasy expectation syndrome." To be clear, clients place high hopes on us. The problem is we can "supersize" expectations to such a degree that not even the most capable advisor in the world could meet them. Health advisors will remind themselves on a regular basis that they are human like every other living, breathing person on the planet. You cannot leap tall buildings in a single bound or hold back declines in the market because a terrorist decided to place a bomb on a plane.

Checking in with our role finds us reviewing accounts, engaging in holistic conversation about clients' lives and goals, staying current with investment platforms offered by the firm for which you work, and communicating clearly how levels of risk can impact investment results. To be in the role as an advisor is to lead clients to discover with you, their best options, help them implement a plan, monitor that plan, and stay in touch with them through the changes in life that come.

Finally, every client meeting or call we make requires us to rekindle the role of advisor. This owning of our call marshals our listening partners, a nurturing presence, and the four C's. To check in using these allies day after day, week after week reminds us we are in the business, bottom line, for one powerful reason: to help people better their lives. Advisors who periodically remind themselves of the role they play in the drama of life and duty, experience a greater sense of fulfillment professionally and personally.

SIGNIFICANT OTHERS

For the life of me, I cannot understand why days become so crowded and demanding. Both Kathie and I have a phrase we use with each other that may resonate with you. When one of us has had an especially demanding day that includes taking more than a few barbs from clients or colleagues, we push the anger down and bring it home. Unaware of this crazy behavior, I inflict the pain on her or she on me and the attacked party says, "I feel like the cat that got kicked at the end of the day." Have you had that feeling? I bet you've even done the kicking at one time or another. I ask again: Is there a reason we avoid or attack significant others when they are the very ones who give us unconditional love and support?

To check in with these special people allows them to take your emotional temperature and check your relational blood pressure. When you ask a loved one to give life feedback, what do they say? How do they say it? Do you find a person who will walk a mile in your shoes?

Kathie has been a loving, and yes, at times challenging presence in my life. My story would not be the narrative it is today had she not been with me for more than two-thirds of my life. We began our life together pulling from south Florida to Louisville, Kentucky a small, two-wheel trailer full of wedding presents, a sleeper sofa, bed, and a rocking chair. Both of us had more courage than sense. Looking back on those early years (Kathie was 19 and I was 22) we knew nothing of commitment, devotion in spite of trial, or maturity. We had no money, no family near us, and no idea of what our futures held, but we had each other. We learned from the very beginning to check in with each other about the big and little things that crossed the bow of our lives. When we vented anger appropriately, offered compassion generously, accepted each other unconditionally, listened to each other intently, and gave good gifts to each other faithfully, life seemed to go a bit better.

Holy matrimony, for all its challenges and imperfections, is still by every measure society's best institution which two people can create and share. How we define marriage has changed, but the ingredients that make this union work are much the same today as they have been generations past. To check in with your spouse and to be a person your spouse can check in with from their side is a gift we couples are wise to give each other. In our marriage, Kathie will ask, "What happened in the markets today?" When I respond with a number, I will then ask her, by profession a residential general contractor, "How was work on your sites?" Those two questions once answered tee up others and lead to what is often a very lively conversation over supper at our kitchen island.

Couples gain strength when they share each other's lives. Learning to listen to a spouse is an excellent training ground for learning how to listen to clients. Men and women who are effective partners in a relationship are often quite effective in connecting with clients. The opposite is true. When we live with people and ignore their pain or turn a deaf ear, we do worse with those we serve. How do I know that? Because if we are unwilling to invest in the life of a person who shares our living space, we are probably incapable of making such an investment in a person we see only twice a year and talk with on the phone another 3 or 4 times in the span of twelve months.

But go deeper. The person with whom you live is a person in whose presence you find a degree of strength, love, understanding, and compassion. Receiving those gifts from an intimate partner can enable you in the advisory work to give those gifts to clients. We are taught to love by being loved. As we learn to listen, we are heard. We learn how to express compassion after we become its recipient. Someone wiser than I once said, "We are smiled into smiling and loved into loving."

Checking in with a life partner extends to others with whom we share a home. Children are amazing; they have much to learn but also much to teach. In the Christian tradition, we remember Jesus who said that "Unless you become as a child, you can never enter the Kingdom of God." Now put aside the religious-spiritual interpretation of that sentence and focus on "become as a child." To check in with children is to get on their level for a few moments to see what they see, hear what they hear, and listen to what they have to say. In my judgment and life experience, children have taught me more than all the philosophers I have read and shown me more love than all the cards Hallmark could ever print.

When you have the opportunity and want to explore a conversation you will probably never forget, ask for some time with a 15-year-old son, daughter, niece, nephew, or the teenager next door. Ask them how they see the world in which we are living. Listen as they tell you about their dreams using words we might not use to express their fears. Get a young adult to imagine what kind of life they want to have when they are 30 and just listen to their hopes and aspirations. When you check in with an adolescent, you dial into a world view that is very different from the one you know as an adult. But seeing what they see and making notes on how they think through issues will only make you a better advisor to that 75-year-old widow who does not know what will happen to her now that her husband of 53 years has died.

Friends with whom we share a common interest can be fascinating individuals for a check in touch. Though not a golfer, I'm told that a person's true character is often revealed in a round of golf. Through 18 holes of drives, iron shots, pitches, and putts, you witness someone who faces and deals with frustration, anger, elation, and integrity. Volunteering with a friend at a soup kitchen or affording a day's labor at a Habitat for Humanity site shows sides of your personality others might not see when you wear a tailored suit and designer tie. Share with a golf or bridge partner, a civic leader or club member a disappointment you've had with a child or a setback you've experienced at work and let them be a friend to you. When you check in with a friend—no matter how shallow or deep, how short or how long the relationship— you learn a bit more about yourself and how others handle life's difficulties. Learning those lessons, you tuck away in your mind a possible tool to help your clients when they are faced with similar challenges.

Finally, if you work with men and women who, like you, run an advisory practice, find ways to spend quality time checking in with them, listening to their struggles, and learning from their successes. Too often we see colleagues as competitors instead of partners. Not long after I got into the financial services business, a seasoned advisor in our office engaged me in conversation about my budding practice. What he was doing was checking in with me, gauging how I was handling the demands of the new job. In that brief but memorable visit—one that the two of us have repeated scores of times since—he told me, "Tim, your competition is not the folks in this office. It's the people at the other firms who are vying for the same clients as you." He went on to encourage me to find in the advisor team around me colleagues who would become friends and enrich the practice I was building from the ground up.

Yes, checking in with those closest to us completes the circle that began with our clients while staying in touch with our role. The caring advisor is not a solitary Paul Bunyan, hewing trees by himself in a dense forest of virgin timber. Quite the opposite:

we are human beings who know that life is best lived in part-nership and relationship with others who, if given the invitation, would gladly plant an entire forest with us. When we check in with clients, we demonstrate that our relationship transcends the monthly statement. When we check in with our role, we remind ourselves that what we do as professionals places a demand on us that deserves our highest attention. As we check in with significant loved ones, we remind ourselves that we are not alone. Checking in is nothing more than adding to the stories in which we find ourselves, staying connected to those stories, finding ways to lead clients based upon their story and the future that story may hold for them. To that work of leadership we now turn as we explore ways advisors pull together much of what they have learned in leading clients to realize the best of the story yet to come.

LOOKING BACK

■   To check in with clients, our role, and ourselves is to be reminded of the softer side of our business that stays in touch with the stories in which we find ourselves.

■   When we check in with clients, we do so not to further the business, but to enhance the relationship.

■   Significant others form a foundation and create focus to who we are. Check in with the people who matter most to you and discover how your work takes on new energy.

Chapter 11

Lead with Purpose

By now, you have come to a greater awareness of yourself and those you serve. We are autonomous, complex individuals who crave connection with others and long for community. The phenomenon witnessed in the rise of Facebook, Twitter, Instagram, LinkedIn, and dozens of other social media platforms convey one message loud and clear: all of us have a need to share our stories with one another. Advisors intuitively know this glaring fact. The challenge, as we have learned, is to shape our practice around this dance of stories between ourselves and those we serve.

So we come now to the last, but surely not the final "role" call. As with any book, the pages run out, the last chapter is written, and we take up what we have learned and weave it into the fabric of our work. You, however, will write many final chapters as you shape your practice and continually support your clients. How you lead with purpose will create a practice model that not only works for you but conveys to clients that higher level of care they need and expect.

For some, leadership is the first and perhaps only topic worth exploring. A president of Harvard University once said, "Give me the right teachers, and everything else will follow. Give me the wrong teachers, and nothing else matters." The same can be said of leadership; when it is in place, everything else follows. A home requires leadership, often shared, but never ignored. Businesses that grow, reach new market share, identify new products, employ and keep the best talent are enterprises fueled by active leadership.

Whether you are in a solo practice or share this good work with partners, clients expect you and those with whom you work to lead.

Some may raise a hand asking how the words "caring" and "leadership" go together. Good question. I contend that without leadership, expressions of care in its varied forms are shallow, even insincere. In the preceding chapters, we have discovered how the stories in which we find ourselves—those of our clients and our own lives—require us to employ focused listening, accurate language, lifelong learning, mindful of the power of presence. This cadence of care crafts client narratives that integrate tangible assets with histories and futures, meaning and purpose. You slowly create vignettes populated with real people whose gains and losses, joys and sorrows unveil the purposeful leadership they need most.

If you have read this far in the book, my guess is you have asked more than once: "Did I sign up for all of this extra work when I passed my licensing exams?" You may have thought CFP®, CPA, Attorney, or Insurance Specialist was mostly about the financial, the legal, and liability issues. All the "advisor" had to do was, well, give advice. To quote from memory a line from the celebrated University of Chicago professor Martin Marty, the only problem with that assumption is "having a complete grip on a half-truth." You are half-right. It's that other half of the work—the half that is more demanding but infinitely more fulfilling and satisfying—that will separate you from all other advisors. With the rise of the "robo-advisor," with legal documents easily downloaded, and consumers believing they can replace an accountant, anyone can find "advice." More than a few studies suggest the millennial generation finds more help online, for less cost than the hands-on services we offer…with one exception.

The robo-advisor—that half-truth side of the work—will not be there for your clients when their parents die. Though a machine can create any number of appropriate asset allocations, that same machine will be silent when clients lose their jobs, when some crisis comes calling with brutal repercussions, or when they simply need to talk to a person face-to-face. In all candor, you can make a living in the financial services business by being the equivalent of a breathing, reacting, living "robo-advisor" and have a job. But if you long to be an advisor who invests in client stories, who exemplifies courage and grace under fire, spend time with your clients when life soars, and when it falls apart. You will be all the better because of it.

To lead with purpose brings together the concepts and behaviors learned in the last ten chapters. What follows is not a summary of those stops along the way, but rather a suggested integration of the themes explored and how combining those areas of client care empowers you to transform your business. You may want to have a pen or pencil handy to make notes in the margins as you read. Though I will lead you through five reflective questions, other questions unique to your practice will come to mind. Jot them down. Let your conscious mind work on possible answers. Allow your subconscious to keep those answers safe. As you do, you will discover that leading with purpose is often not directive but suggestive, intuitive rather than analytical. Let us see where these five questions take us.

Do our stories matter that much?

When you scan the relationships in your present book of business, my guess is you already know quite a bit about your clients' life stories. You may know something about their families of origin and the communities in which they were reared. A few or more extended family members may be their friends in the community. Clients you have served for five years or more have added color and texture to what you first learned about them. In those intervening years, you may have been with ten or more clients when a parent died. You may have attended some or all of those funerals. I would imagine you have witnessed clients' children graduate from college, leave home for military service, marry and start families of their own.

Over time, we learn bits and pieces of our clients' stories because we are tuned in and aware of their changing circumstances. Do client stories really matter? You tell me if knowing about multi-generation mental illness concerns would be important when first working with a 40-year-old business owner who seems overly anxious about anything having to do with money. Tell me the value of knowing that two of your clients shared a common grandfather who was a decorated World War II hero and went on after the war to become a member of the state legislature. Would it matter if you knew the person sitting in front of you had survived childhood cystic fibrosis and may still be vulnerable to its pernicious respiratory assault? Though some would look the other way, would knowing a client was abused physically or sexually by a step-parent, neighbor, family member, or other trusted adult make a difference in how you hear that client's story?

Recall with me our voyage into language and those conversational punctuation marks. Narratives of all our lives arrive at similar endings. Some of those endings—death, graduation, marriage, first birth, first home—have a full period at the end and are rarely repeated. We graduate from high school once, we buy a "first home," we marry for the "first" time, we welcome our "first" child into the world, and yes, we die once. Other narratives end with commas, colons, exclamation points, and more than a few question marks. It is those stories that linger on in memory, shaping and coloring how we understand who we are that need another hearing. Yes, knowing the stories that go beyond a balance sheet, bequests in a will, a tax return, or the placing of a life insurance policy can radically alter a client's ability to make important, life-affecting decisions about money, values, and relationships.

If you want to have what might be the most self-revelatory experience, tiptoe into the story approach with just one or two new clients. Ask if they would visit with you for no other reason than your need to know them better. Use the suggested interview questions in the Appendix. Better yet, commit to memory the broad categories within that document freeing you to be more conversational with your clients. Get them to talk about their childhood, what money means to them, how they met their spouse, what their parents taught them about life, values, work, and success. Ask open-ended questions. Take notes. At the end of the hour, when they have said all they can and need to say, ask "I suppose you are wondering why I wanted you to visit with me today and listen to your life stories." They will probably nod or say, "It has crossed our minds." Continue, "I wanted this time with you because your story matters to me." Take ten minutes and share with them two or three brief stories from your own past revealing how those experiences changed your understanding of money, values, family, and the future. End the visit by saying, "You have asked me to come alongside you and your family as an advisor. I take that invitation seriously and am humbled by it. If we are going to do our very best work together, I must know your stories and, in turn, you will come to know many of my own. We'll learn more about each other as we work together. But today, you gave me a huge gift and for that, I am grateful."

Do stories matter? As my wife has reminded me through the reading of every word and chapter in this book, "Every life crisis has financial implications." As she explored that sentence with me, windows opened and the lights went on in the corridors of my mind. I realized every experience from birth to death touches in some way on the issue of money. Learn the stories of your clients. Come to know and value your own story, both its successes and failures. Then put them together as you implement care, expressing support for the people you serve.

Does the client expect this level of engagement?

I am sure there are clients who do not expect nor do they want you to know that much about them. Some clients are closed books that neither you nor the Almighty can open. That said, I believe the overwhelming majority of your clients may not be able to voice this expectation, but they will be grateful for your concern for them and those they love. Not too many weeks ago, one of our senior clients suffered a debilitating fall at home. That fall has taken a devastating physical and emotional toll on this woman whom I have known for more than 25 years. Her husband is in relatively good health, but their two children live in distant states.

In speaking with her daughter who called me from New Mexico, we talked about her mother's resilience, her incredible energy level, and the reality check this fall and its consequences had taken on her. Then the daughter said, "I told mom today that not only is she getting excellent medical care, but she has the only financial advisor I've known who makes hospital visits!" I was glad to be on the other end of the phone so she couldn't see me blush, but what a compliment. Since then, I have visited with this client several times and will continue to connect with her until she makes as full a recovery as is possible.

The non-business side of my relationship with this senior couple has allowed me to accumulate dozens of stories from the more than 60 years they have spent together: their families of origin and parents value systems, career changes, illness, rearing children, and other memories both dear and painful. When my client fell and was admitted to the hospital, I knew where her children lived, I knew the personalities involved, I understood nuanced details about this couple's marriage and relationship with each other, and I acted in ways that were consistent with being their advisor and confidant.

The time to learn your clients' stories is not when you get a phone call from someone telling you they are in the hospital, were involved in a life-threatening accident, or received a less-than-positive diagnosis from a physician. Yes, you can go to the hospital, make the call expressing concern, and ask to visit with them when they deem it appropriate. But you will not bring to that meeting, that visit, that conversation the wealth of information you would bring if you knew that client's story. Failing to be aware of the sensitive chapters that impact all the others diminishes your role and robs clients of what could be the best you have to offer them.

Do clients expect us to be invested in their stories, aware of so much of their lives they may have hidden from others? The answer is probably, "No," but oh how they enjoy the attention and value your time and energy. Why not ask the question of your own practice. What ten clients would most welcome my having a meaningful, story-focused conversation with them? You might receive such positive feedback that the list grows to include the majority of your clients. When you surprise a client with a concentrated level of care and personal attention, you form an impenetrable bond.

Do they expect this deeper level of engagement? No, because in their experience, advisors have been, for the most part, single-minded and concerned only about the investment side of the business. Advisors must know their clients to a certain degree, however, beyond the information learned in that initial fact-finding mission, the relationship has a period that looks like our office door. I have learned something that is not surprising both in my practice as a minister and financial advisor. I have discovered people value this deeper, warmer, caring approach more than even they believed they would. I can almost hear them say, "I have never known a professional who cares so much about me and the people I love."

Why am I reluctant to deepen relationships with my clients?

The most inaccurate picture of a leader I can think of is a man or woman standing in front of people giving directions. A similar inaccurate picture is a pseudo-leader who sits behind a desk creating directives to subordinates about the work that needs to be done. Managing by memo does not, has not, and will never be a part of an effective leader's behavior. *Wrong, inaccurate,* and *unhealthy* are the words that come to mind when I find myself standing before images like that!

I can only speak for myself, but the number one reason I am reluctant to take a client relationship to a more profound level is the time and transparency it demands of me to do so. In a word, if you choose to invest more in your clients' stories by becoming more aware of your own, you will have to go to a place of vulnerability many are not willing to go. That level of self-disclosure shuts down some and threatens most. And yet, that candidness and transparency, when offered us, only draws us closer to others.

One of the best conversations you can have is the sharing of a funny story from your life. When the joke is on me, I laugh again and realize others are laughing, not at me, but with me. When you disclose a funny or embarrassing moment from your past, what happens? Almost immediately, the person with whom you are speaking relaxes and says, "That is so funny! It reminds me of something that happened to me a couple of years ago." Your story opens the door, granting permission for the other person to share. I have been in various sized groups where 30 minutes passed before we realized we had been enjoying each other's company unlike any time before. Sharing something about yourself that touches a common chord in others not only warms the client to the story but also to you.

Why might advisors be reluctant to use this approach? It takes an investment of time in the relationship, which, in my experience, has always rewarded me with more assets to manage, more challenges to solve, and more introductions to new clients. The people you and I serve will gladly share your name with a friend, family member, neighbor, or business associate when they know that person will be treated well. On the other hand, a client who believes we are exclusively focused on the money, the deal, the investment product, the plan, will see us as nothing more than financial services salespersons. I can think of no easier introduction an existing client could make to the work you and I do than to say to someone they know, "Not only is my advisor good at what he does, but he has been there for me and my family when we went through a very difficult time."

Perhaps we are simply afraid of engaging others in this way because we believe it's "all or nothing." Would you agree that using some of these concepts might make a difference in your relationships with clients? Why not try one or two of your choosing and then decide? It could be our reluctance is found in the time required to learn these concepts well. A pesky voice inside me suggests we hesitate to approach our work in this way because we don't know how to get started. Try this: slowly but deliberately invest the time and transparency to go this way with a few clients until you feel more comfortable. My conviction is that, in time, you will not begin any new relationship without sharing your story and learning the stories these new clients bring to you, which leads to the obvious fourth question.

What is the payoff?

But will this improve the bottom line of my business? Is there a financial and professional silver lining to approaching my work this way? The old cliché is memorable, but again, only a half-truth: "Time is money." Yes, it is if your focus is exclusively on billable hours, policies placed, portfolio fees collected, and all the administrative demands checked off. We have all at times found ourselves lost in a forest of dense trees that block out the sun, thick underbrush scraping our legs, and sounds innocent and threatening raising the hair on our necks. The business jungle is so inviting when we tuck a license in our pocket, set up an office, create a list of potential clients, and wait for the phone to ring. We can—and many advisors do—get so lost in doing business we lose sight of the "North Star" of why our business matters.

More than a few of us have been patients of physicians who are highly educated and board certified, but who have little or no bedside manner. Visits to the office are filled with small-talk and "tell me why you're here today" questions. Such a physician pokes here and listens there, has us cough a few times while she places a cold stethoscope on our back, reviews the chart, scribbles out a prescription, and then walks out. At the front office, we are told: "That will be $50 for your co-pay; cash or credit card?" We leave asking ourselves, "What just happened?"

We forget that our clients have the same intuitive instincts we have. Like us, they know when the relationship smells like a "business only" air freshener. Let's be candid. All of the advisory professions are requiring more and more forms to sign and compliance issues to satisfy. The mere act of doing the business side of the job can be overwhelming, confusing, and yes, frustrating. For that reason alone, advisors in every field must find ways to re-humanize the tasks before us not only to convey a genuine concern for those we serve but to know what matters to them.

So what is the payoff to being an engaged, storytelling, care-centric advisor? In order to answer the question, imagine with me a 200-acre family farm that, year after year, produces a crop sold at the market while simultaneously managing a dairy with 80 Holstein cows. Look at half of the farm devoted to the herd of cows that includes a five-acre section from which the farmer grows a very lucrative cash crop. These 100 acres of your business are the purely transactional product-deliverable "land" from which you make a living. The cows and this small cash crop pay the bills. Having spent eight years of my young adulthood in Kentucky in the late 1970s, early 1980s, I learned that most farmers in the state planted corn, milked cows, sowed winter wheat after the corn was harvested, and grew a cash crop—burley tobacco.

Advisors make their money from the business side of their 200 acres. That's where the contracts are signed, the portfolios invested, policies issued, and from which fees and commissions flow to create an income. Without these 100 acres (half the farm) no matter how fertile the other acreage is, the farmer cannot stay in business. Let me be clear. We cannot survive in any advisory business without creating an income. When asked, "Why are you in business?" the first answer is always, "To make money." Everyone deserves to be compensated for their labor, their expertise, and the quality of services offered. See no head in the sand with me on this issue. The financial payoff to being an advisor is not only expected but required if any of us plan to stay in business. But that's only half the farm!

The other half of the farm makes possible that money-making, business enterprise on which we are paid. It includes 90 acres planted in corn to feed the dairy herd, two acres for a home, barn, and space to park equipment, and eight acres here and there lost to trees, a creek that flows through the property, and other ground that cannot be cultivated. The corn harvested off the 90 acres is not sold on the market but fed to the cows! Some of that corn, in mid-summer, is ground into silage, as the milk production falls off because of warm weather. The other half of the stalk is harvested, and ground into feed for the approaching winter. This book has focused on the half of the farm that makes possible the keeping of the herd and growing the cash crop. When farmers have a good year growing corn and tobacco, the herd is happy, the family has groceries on the table, and in the heart of a cold Kentucky winter, the family has enough extra money to head to Florida for a much needed and deserved vacation.

Is there a payoff to being a caring advisor? In my judgment, based on more than 30 years of walking through all manner of life experiences with men, women, children, teenagers, couples, families, business owners, seniors, the sick, the shut-in, the dying, the abandoned, the lonely, and the confused, there is no better way to build an advisory business than being a caring, trusted professional. Taking up these tools and incrementally, thoughtfully integrating them into a practice enriches the relationship while growing the business. Advisors who do not become more present to their clients, for any number of what they deem good reasons, may make a living, but they will miss the joy of creating a life full of greater professional satisfaction.

What if you forward-imagined your advisory story with me for just a few sentences? What would your relationships look like five years from now? Imagine a couple who sat with you just four years ago sharing chapters from their lives. During those invested hours, you learned about the husband, at nine years of age, losing his father to cancer while his mother worked two jobs to keep the family fed and housed. During this same conversation, you discovered the wife's family owned a large manufacturing plant in a Midwestern city that, during her childhood, was the city's largest employer. But then the second world war came and most of the men in that plant were drafted, leaving her family's business in a very difficult place. You absorbed the feeling, the language, the emotion in those stories. You came to understand both this man and this woman in ways you could never have imagined had you not gone there with them.

Now, six years into your advisory relationship with them, four years after sitting with them through the telling of their life stories, she is losing her battle with cancer and he seems as lost in this world as the survivor of a shipwreck on a raft in the middle of the ocean. Do you think those invested hours four years ago was worth it now? Can you see out there in the future how knowing so much about this one client couple would help you at this very tender time be a nurturing presence to their adult children and grandchildren? Would you not sense deep satisfaction from having made sure their advance directives were current and letters of authorization signed permitting you to discuss with their children financial and/or legal matters? The answer to all of these questions is obvious.

The payoff to being a caring advisor cannot be quantified on a balance sheet or totaled with a calculator. Leading with purpose calls advisors to look beyond where the business is to where the business might best go, always with people and their stories at the very heart of it all. Imagine your practice changed because you decided to take this jaunt with those who compensate you for the work you do. They long to learn more about you because you have delivered more to them than anyone ever has. Imagine that!

Can I do this?

To lead with purpose requires the answering of this competency question. No certifying board, trusted colleague or even intimate friend can answer this nagging question pinging at our souls: "Do I have what it takes?" You may pass the state bar and be admitted to the practice at your community's most prestigious firm and still not know in your soul you can do what the diploma and certificate on the wall say you are licensed to do. This work, taking up the mantle of the caring advisor, is work whose competency comes by incrementally integrating care, compassion, listening, learning, language, presence, and understanding into one's practice. That takes time. But most of all, it takes courage.

Someone far wiser than I penned a sentence that may well capture the challenge we face. Memorize the following seven words: "The hardest step is at the start." For years now, we have rented our home to patrons attending the Masters® held in Augusta, Georgia the first full week of April. Right after the first of the year, I look at our garage in need of a bit of attention and say to myself, "I think I'll clean up the garage later." And then February morphs into March and that big week in April is almost here. So on a Saturday in mid-March, I put on my work clothes, back out the cars, and begin tidying up our garage. I dust off the shelves, toss out unwanted junk, and finally mop the garage floor. After about 15 minutes of work, I say under my breath, "This isn't nearly as difficult as I thought it would be," and soon, an hour or so later, the task is done. I look at a magnificently clean, reordered garage and beam with pride at the great job I finally did.

The hardest step in becoming a caring advisor is at the start. Now focus on the word "incrementally." No matter the task before us, we take first starter steps by incrementally adding caring behaviors and thoughtful questions, and listening with genuine sensitivity. We make the decision to ask multi-layered questions that throw open windows to the client's world. The start comes when we have add to an expected review a 20-minute block asking them to unpack some specific moment in their lives. Starts are not leaps nor are they transformations. They are tentative beginnings, baby steps, knowing we may stumble but we step out nonetheless.

Starting anything requires being intentional. With that in mind, here are a few entry questions you can ask clients to get them talking about themselves:

■ We have now worked together for a couple of years. I have always wanted to ask you about the place you called home when you were a child. Tell me where you grew up and something memorable about your family?

■ A few minutes ago, you made mention of a transition taking place at work. How do you feel about that? Was there a time when you were growing up when one of your parents went through a similar change at work?

■ We've talked from time to time about the importance you are placing on educating your children. Would you tell me the value your parents placed on education when you were growing up?

■ I remember from our last conversation you mentioned the declining health of a family member. How is she doing? We all eventually have to face our own mortality. (*I would say the following from my own life experience. You have your own story to tell.*) I struggled with my own mortality when my father lost his battle with a rare blood disease. Going with him to the precipice of death and seeing in him a living faith as he faced his transition has helped me value my own life asking what legacy I will leave my children. Have you thought about that during this time of change in your family?

Possible story-starting, leading questions number in the hundreds or more. Can you do this? You can if you prepare for these conversations pro-actively. Prior to these first visits, jot down questions and make them conversational. Be mindful of your presence, posture, and voice inflection. Ask if you might make a few notes as they talk. Briefly, jot a note, remembering to keep your focus on the client.

We all have a "start" story to tell from a time in our life when we first dove into a leadership role. The first church I served as pastor was a rural congregation in the heart of Kentucky's rolling southern farmland. In assuming the pastoral role, I knew that eventually I would have to officiate at a funeral; something I had not done before. Ten months into my work, two parishioners died within hours of each other. Now I had two funerals to lead, both on the same day! Those individuals could not have been more different. Though I had been their pastor and was trained to conduct a funeral, I had never presided over one. I was green, uncertain, and somewhat terrified. I had no idea how I would get through the days between their deaths and those funerals without a huge amount of divine help. Having never officiated, much less spoken at a funeral, I walked down the basement stairs of the parsonage and sat at my desk. I realized the only way the sermons would get written and the funerals planned was for me to start with the first word.

Fortunately, a couple of years earlier as required reading for a seminary course, I had a book on how to plan a funeral. I read those chapters with suggested outlines for eulogies and sermons, put down the book, and began making notes. The orders for the service came together within 30 minutes. To be frank, there are but a few ways to structure a funeral! That helped. But I had to write sermons for each of the deceased. With a pen in hand and a legal pad in my lap, I started jotting down everything I remembered about these two people from my relationships with them over the previous 10 months. Sad to say, I knew the woman far better than I knew the man, who died a near pauper with no children and few family members. He was a loner; my few attempts to reach him were unsuccessful. This man seemed lost in a very lonely, painful world. Notes for his sermon would have to wait.

The woman, on the other hand, was active in the church. She had family both in the area and others but a few hours' drive away.

The words, adjectives, emotions, and memories of this woman and her devotion to God and others seemed to flow from my hand to the yellow pad of paper in my lap. An hour went by. Soon, I had the sermon together for her. Then the harder work began. I picked up the phone, called the deceased man's cousin and found answers to some of my questions. In that conversation, I asked a question I have since asked hundreds of families preparing a funeral for their loved ones. "Can you tell me a story or two about this person that captures much of who they were and what they loved?" This cousin not only told me a story, he told me more than five stories that helped me understand the man I would bury the following day.

The question of competence is always pacing in our minds. At times, we rightly question our abilities knowing that the task before us is better done by another professional or perhaps not done at all. If, however, we keep the stories within that life in focus, our work becomes not only easier but infinitely more fulfilling. We take up the tools of the caring advisor one instrument, one conversation, one story, one visit, one question, one act of kindness at a time. As one of my mentors in the business taught me in the first weeks of building my practice, "This work is a marathon, not a sprint." We spend time with them both during scheduled reviews and in those moments when life falls apart. To ask "Can I do this?" seems to find our eyes staring at the face of a very steep mountain. Incrementally, thoughtfully, and with a staunch determination to become that caring, supportive presence to clients, you can and will climb that mountain, no matter how steep.

The work before us starts, ends, and will always be a story in which we live, move and have our very being. One day, we all will die out of the grand picture leaving behind stories those who loved us will narrate. In the telling of those stories, life in its splendor seems to happen all over again. Becoming a living, caring, understanding presence to our clients does not happen overnight. This work of being an advisor is a marathon that has no end because, in reality, it has no definable beginning. At the end of the day, year, or career, clients will clean out their desks, remove a few pictures from the wall and credenza, carry two or three boxes of office "stuff" to the car and drive home only to step into what may be a retirement story. The caring advisor makes that trip as well, but does so with an imaginary U-Haul trailer of stories, memories, and moments that s/he shared with clients that not only made work better, but infused a career with gifts of love, compassion, and faith no license or title can capture.

So lead with purpose. Take up this good and noble work. Invest more of yourself in the lives of those you serve one encounter at a time. Risk being misunderstood by some but loved and appreciated by most. See yourself as a caring, competent professional whose advisory story has others at its very center. Imagine now what size U-Haul you may need to reserve when, one day, you pack up your office and start writing another chapter. What has motivated me to write every sentence in this book is the hope that you will so fully live the magic of your own story and those of your clients that their lives and yours will be enriched beyond measure. Go there. Discover no higher or more fulfilling joy than having others say of you, "My life is so much better because my advisor took the time to understand, know, and love me and those I love in ways that have transformed our lives and our future."

Acknowledgments

The book you hold in your hands is a work that has been in development for more than four decades, if not a lifetime. My story, though unique and unrepeatable, is an evolving narrative of people, places, and passions. Family members, together and separately, have contributed love, encouragement, correction, support, and wisdom. No man or woman is an island. We are wondrously connected to each other. Throughout my 40-year professional career, I have known extraordinary individuals who served as mentors, role models, associates, and friends. Their investments are priceless; their friendship forever. An eight-year, two-degree seminary education followed by serving as pastor to five congregations sowed the seeds of learning and experience that have yielded a bountiful harvest. From polio to music, marriage to ministry and the major and minor chords in between, my life's piano concerto has been remarkable and full of joy.

To list the names of people who have played their part, measure after measure, would be impossible. I must, however, mention the following because, without them, *Cadence of Care* would have remained but an idea lost in a crowded room elbowed out by others vying for a hearing. Because of my firm's compliance restrictions, I cannot name the colleagues with whom I am affiliated who inspired me to dream of and write this book. The manager who hired me, associates in the office, and especially my active and retired partners became and still are sources of inspiration and insight. Before I imagined the first sentence, the firm provided, through its intranet blog, an avenue to begin exploring this unique advisory approach. Our national training center has been a venue in which I have trotted out many of the book's concepts before a live audience. One of our firm's most respected leaders became a champion for this approach to client care. I trust he knows how much he means to me and how grateful I am for his advocacy and blessing. My present manager, senior firm management, compliance and legal personnel have thoughtfully protected and guided me and the book's content while freeing both, leading to its publication. I could not ask for more generous support.

Colleagues in the larger financial services world have been trusted partners in sharpening both thought and writing. I offer heartfelt thanks to Bob Doll of Nuveen Asset Management for writing the Foreword. Bob is not only a dear friend but a man of uncommon stature and respect on Wall Street. He is a genuinely loving and affirming, gracious and humble human being. Thank you, Bob, for saying "Yes." Don Connelly, to whom all of us in the business owe so much, encouraged me to pursue this project with focus and passion. I continue to sit at Don's feet to learn how best to show the value a trusted advisor brings to clients. He is without peer as a mentor, teacher, storyteller, and advocate for advisors.

Parishioners and clients alike have offered me their life stories, struggles, disappointments, joys, failures, sorrows, and triumphs. They did not know it at the time, but they have been the best teachers of human behavior and nature I have had. The high compliment they paid me is the sharing of their most intimate selves, asking me to be their friend, confidant, minister, and advisor. To sit with another in the sanctuary of the soul is to be in the presence of the holy. Those many invitations have not been lost in the shifting sands of time.

Others who have inspired my journey begin with Dr. Marc Miller. In the book's infancy, Marc was Dean of Augusta University's Hull College of Business. He has since become Dean of the School of Business, Henderson State University in Arkadelphia, Arkansas. Marc granted me an embarrassing amount of time early on as I shared the book's focus and approach. Throughout its writing, he offered much wisdom, always seasoned with grace. Much of the energy to wrestle with embryonic ideas and to keep writing is due in no small measure to Marc's investment. His interest in seeing this book written and published is only exceeded by his insistence that its concepts find a larger audience. Other friends with whom I shared dozens of fledgling thoughts and those who read portions of the manuscript offering thoughtful feedback include Dr. Jeffrey Flowers, Rev. Paulwyn Boliek, David Steele, Dr. John Church, Ted Hussey, Dr. Matthew Rich, Charlene Sizemore, Dr. Rodger Murchison, Maj. Gen. Perry M. Smith (Ret.), Dr. Robert Seaberg, Shell Berry, Steve Sanders, Dr. Allen Walworth, Martha Jean McHaney, Wyck Knox, Dr. Steve Hobbs, and Dr. Doug Pryor.

For nearly 30 years, Bill Curry has been a soul-centered, devoted friend. Bill and I first met when I was pastor of Calvary Baptist Church adjacent to the campus of the University of Alabama where he was head football coach. Providence brought us together at a time in both of our lives when we needed a trusted friend. He confessed to me that Georgia Tech did not focus on English, but his engineering education majored on precision. His reading of the manuscript is the most recent example of the coaching-mentoring bond we have enjoyed across the years. Bill and Carolyn Curry's friendship is a singular love gift to my family and me.

Perhaps the most vexing, chronic challenge facing a writer is time and uncluttered space to write sentences that eventually end up altered or deleted. As the book moved from conception and gestation to its first gasping breaths, the Becton family offered Kathie and me the better part of a week at their mountain home near Highlands, North Carolina. Those days at over 3,000 feet, gazing at Whiteside Mountain in the distance, gave me a venue to advance the book's content and structure. Kathie would read a chapter, we would discuss it, and then I would return to my laptop to make the changes. Those were special days filled with creativity without which this baby would not have been born.

Someone has rightly observed that to write is to re-write. Over the last year, I have written and re-written every smidgen of the book several times. But the best work I have done has been under the guidance of my amazing and gifted editor, Melanie Calloway. Kathie and I met Melanie and her husband Anthony when we with them attended the Earl Klugh Jazz Festival at The Sanctuary, Kiawah Island in November 2015. We introduced ourselves to each other and shared the usual question, "What do you do?" Melanie said she was a talent scout. I thought, "jazz festival, talent scout" and replied, "So you're looking to represent musicians here at the festival?" "No," she said, "I represent motivational speakers." Not only did I learn Melanie is a talent scout. She is an exceptional editor. This book would not be anything close to what you now hold in your hand without her many labors of love. We share a very special, warm, working relationship forged in the fire of her incredibly gifted personality and professional expertise. She has been and continues to be a priceless gift.

The last reader took the manuscript to the mat looking for those annoying things like misspellings and grammatical errors. Dennis Sodomka, our local newspaper's retired senior editor, became the final set of eyes flagging a typo here and a grammatical train wreck there. The two of us share a 25-year friendship made even stronger by his critical and keen literary eye across every page. Thank you does not seem quite enough. The next Bordeaux is on me!

Heartfelt gratitude goes out to Catherine Staton and her team at Stroud & Hall Publishers for their willingness to take the manuscript and bring it to print. From our first conversation, Catherine has held my hand, guiding Melanie and me through the many steps that take a work from a digital file to the beautifully crafted volume you hold in your hands. To all these devoted friends, colleagues, and partners I owe unbounded gratitude for their generous contributions, aware that what flaws remain are mine alone.

Family is and perhaps has always been a slippery, ever-changing institution. A giving reality at its core, our families love us into life, breathing into our souls what it means to love and be loved. My children—Nathan, Justin, and Lindsey—and our two daughters-in-law, Rebekah and Sonal, along with our five grandchildren, Griffin, Aviana, Roland, Raya, and Kanon have given me more love, inspiration, joy, and grace than any father could possibly imagine. When my life modulates into a minor key, being around them quickly transposes what was darkness into light, struggle into exhilaration, uncertainty into hope. No father or grandfather could imagine more love than I continue to receive from these incredibly beautiful human beings.

Finally, I must thank the love of my life, my wife of over 40 years, who has encouraged me in this good work from day one. Kathie Owings is many things to many people. She is a gifted and incredibly creative homebuilder, a first-class business woman, an amazing mother and grandmother, a trusted friend to many and my lifelong soulmate. We have come to this fifth decade of our life together not without a few scars, many joyous memories, bumps along the way, disappointments, sorrows, gains and losses of our own. Those temporary moments of pain cannot obviate or eclipse the bright and warm love in which we have lived. She is God's gift to God's world. I have had the rare and delightful privilege of sharing life's journey with her as my wife, lover, partner, and best friend. This book, sweetheart, is dedicated to you, my best teacher, mentor, critic and muse.

Endnotes

1. Throughout the book, I use *he, she, him, her,* and *his* inter-changeably. The English language, and all language to some extent, has this gender awareness embedded in it that vexes writers of all literary genres. Occasionally, I will use S/he to remind us of this seemingly unsolvable challenge.

2. (Dearborn Trade Publishing, 2000), pp. 54-75.

3. *Man's Search for Meaning* (Boston: Beacon Press, 2006), p. 66.

4. My commitment to what clergy call priestly confidentiality is uncompromised throughout the book. Though I have at times used the real names of people I have served, all situations and conversations are composites of interactions with others for over 40 years.

5. See Walter J. Ong, *Orality and Literacy: The Technologizing of the Word* (Metheun & Co., Ltd, 1982) for an engaging study of language and how writing changed and continues to change communication.

6. From an interview aired on National Public Radio (October 13, 2013), http://www.wfdd.org/story/alan-rickman-cbgb-and-importance-listening.

7. From Lamar Alexander's eulogy of Senator Howard Baker, July 1, 2014, as archived in *The Congressional Record*, pp. 54235-54236.

8. Ralph Nader video interview—Academy of Achievement (February 16, 1991). Retrieved November 25, 2015, http://www.achievement.org/autodoc/page/nad0int-1.

9. Dale Carnegie, in his classic *How to Win Friends and Influence People*, Rev. Sub edition (Simon & Schuster, 1981), pp. 63-70, may have been the first to suggest the powerful connection created by a smile.

10. The classic study on the five stages of grief is that of Elisabeth Kubler-Ross, *On Death and Dying*. Reprint edition. (Simon & Schuster, 2011). Denial is grief's first stage followed by anger, bargaining, depression, and acceptance.

11. (HarperCollins, 1993), p. 2.

12. In his insightful book, *A Week from Next Tuesday* (Wipf & Stock Publishers, 2013) Matthew A. Rich explores from a Christian faith perspective the difference between happiness and joy. Advisors reach new levels of client understanding when they distinguish between the two, embracing the goal of helping clients find joy's more lasting gift as an asset in achieving life balance.

13. (Random House, 2015).

Reading List

Anthony, Mitch and Scott West. *Storyselling for Financial Advisors: How Top Producers Sell.* Dearborn Financial Publishing, 2000.

Blanchard, Kenneth and S. Truett Cathy. *The Generosity Factor: Discover the Joy of Giving Your Time, Talent, and Treasure.* Zondervan, 2002.

Bolles, Richard. *What Color Is Your Parachute? 2016: A Practical Manual for Job-Hunters and Career-Changers* Random House, 2015.

Broughton, Philip Delves. *The Art of the Sale.* Penguin Books, 2008.

Buber, Martin. *I and Thou.* Walter Kaufmann, trans. Touchstone, 1970.

Buechner, Frederick. *Wishful Thinking: A Seeker's ABC.* HarperOne, 1993.

Buford, Bob. *Halftime: Changing Your Gameplan from Success to Significance.* HarperCollins, 2011.

Carnegie, Dale. *How to Win Friends and Influence People.* Rev. Sub Edition. Simon and Schuster, 1981.

Carson, Ron. *Tested in the Trenches: A 9-Step Plan for Building and Sustaining a Million-Dollar Financial Services Practice.* Dearborn Trade Publications, 2005.

Curry, Bill. *Ten Men You Meet in the Huddle: Lessons from a Football Life.* Random House, 2009.

Doidge, Norman. *The Brain That Changes Itself: Stories of Personal Triumph from the Frontiers of Brain Science.* Penguin Books, 2007.

Ferrazzi, Keith. *Never Eat Alone: And Other Secrets to Success, One Relationship at a Time.* Currency-Doubleday, 2005.

Frankl, Victor. *Man's Search for Meaning.* Boston: Beacon Press, 2006.

Grant, Adam. *Give and Take: Why Helping Others Drives Our Success.* Penguin Books, 2013.

Iyengar, Sheena. *The Art of Choosing.* Hachette Book Group, 2010.

Kubler-Ross, Elizabeth. *On Death and Dying.* Reprint Edition. Simon & Schuster, 2011.

Murchison, Rodger. *Guide for Grief.* David Crum Media, 2012.

Murray, Nick. *The New Financial Advisor.* 2001.

Ong, Walter. *Orality and Literacy: The Technologizing of the Word.* Routledge, 1982.

Peale, Norman Vincent. *The Power of Positive Thinking.* New York: Prentice-Hall, 1952.

Rich, Matthew K. *A Week from Next Tuesday.* Wipf & Stock, 2013.

Ryan, Michael F. *The Last Freedom: A Novel on the Real-Life Adventure of Dr. Viktor Frankl.* iUniverse, 2008.

Smith, Perry M. and Jeffrey W. Foley. *Rules & Tools for Leaders: From Developing Your Own Skills to Running Organizations of Any Size.* Penguin Group, 2013.

Vessenes, Peter and Katherine. *Building Your Multi-Million Dollar Practice.* Kaplan Publishing, 2005.

Westberg, Granger E. *Good Grief.* (50th Anniversary Edition). Fortress Press, 2010.

Crafting a Life Story

Name: _____

Date of Birth: _____

Place of Birth: _____

PARENTAL INFLUENCE

Father's Name: _____

Date of Birth: _____

Place of Birth: _____

Education (circle highest)
High School   *College*   *Graduate degree* _____

Employed? Y N
If yes, where? _____

Retired? Y N
If retired, when? _____

Is your father living? Y N
If deceased, when? _____

Three words that capture your father:

_____   _____   _____

Mother's Name: _____

Date of Birth: _____

Place of Birth: _____

Education (circle highest)
High School   *College*   *Graduate degree* _____

Employed? Y N
If yes, where? _____

Retired? Y N
If retired, when? _____

Is your mother living? Y N
If deceased, when? _____

Three words that capture your mother:

_____   _____   _____

Parents' Marital status?

Father: Divorced/Single   Remarried   Widowed/Single

Mother: Divorced/Single   Remarried   Widowed/Single

If one or both parents remarried, describe your relationship with your
step-parent(s)

_____

_____

_____

_____

_____

HISTORIC MATRIX

Where did you grow up? _____

What did the United States look like to you in those early years?

_____

_____

_____

_____

_____

Do you have brothers and sisters?   Y   N
Where are you in the birth order? _____

Are you close to your siblings?   Y   N

If you have siblings, who is the "go-to" brother or sister when you need support?

■   Why do you turn to that particular sibling?
■   What one-character trait do you admire in that sibling?

Focus on your life at age nine

■   How was your home heated and cooled?
■   Where was the home located? Rural Urban Suburban International
■   Talk about one or two friends you had in the fourth or fifth grade.
■   Can you recall a time when you were frightened or felt in physical danger?

■   What did the following words mean when you heard them from your
     parents?
Education
Politics
The arts
Neighbors
Work
Saving
Recreation
Faith
Happiness

During your teenage years . . .

■   Did you develop an interest in sports? Music? School Club? Hobby?
■   Who taught you how to drive?
■   Talk about conversations with parent(s) that looked beyond high
     school
     ○   College
     ○   Military
     ○   Trade school or a job
■   Were you involved in drugs, alcohol, or gangs during this time?
■   What career did you envision for yourself when you were 16?
     ○   Did you share your dream with someone you trusted?
     ○   Did you know what it would take to reach that career goal?
     ○   How did you imagine you would get there?
■   Did parents counsel you about finding a life partner?
     ○   What was their advice?
     ○   Did you consider their counsel seriously?

YOUNG ADULT LIFE

Did you attend college?   Y   N
Where? _____

What was your major? _____ Graduation year? _____

Where you in a sorority/fraternity?   Y   N
     Was that positive?   Y   N

Talk about your first post-college job

- How did you discover the opportunity?
- Was it related to your course of study?
- What attracted you to that first job?

SIGNIFICIANT OTHERS

1. Family
Marital Status: Single   Married   Divorced   Widowed

If married, how did you meet your spouse?

_____

_____

Where and when were you married? _____

_____

Talk about your spouse/partner
- What is your spouse's education level?
- If work is outside the home, where and what?
- What are three words that capture your spouse's personality or character?

Do you have children? If so, how many and what are their ages?

_____

- What is most important to you as a parent?
- Talk about your children—their interests, gifts and personalities
- If they are in school, what subjects do they enjoy most?

What are your dreams for your children?

_____

_____

_____

_____

_____

What keeps you up at night when you think about your children and
their futures?

_____

_____

_____

2. Friends, Work Associates, Neighbors, Faith Community Ties

Name: _____

Place: _____

Influences: _____

Memories: _____

List at least four more individuals outside family who have shaped your
story.

_____

_____

_____

_____

OTHER CONVERSATIONAL TOPICS

What do you and your spouse consider fun things to do together?

_____

What does money mean to each of you?

_____

Describe the conversational tone present when you and your spouse talk about money.

_____

Are there topics you would rather not talk about with your spouse?

_____

Are there real or potential threats to your well-being or that of your family?

_____

What do faith and/or having a faith community mean to you?

_____

What does the phrase "healthy lifestyle" mean to you?

_____

How do you feel about your work, career, profession, or employer?

_____

When you hear the word "retire" or "retirement", what comes to mind?

_____

Circle three (3) of the people below you would consider a "life advisor."

Spouse	Brother	Sister	Mother
Father	Mother-in-law	Father-in-law	Uncle
Aunt	Friend	Co-worker	Neighbor
Minister	Priest	Rabbi	Imam
Financial Advisor	Insurance Agent	CPA	Attorney
Business Partner	Physician	Boss	Supervisor
Professor	Teacher	Coach	Counselor

Tim Owings, Ph.D., CFP®

After nearly 25 years serving as senior pastor to five congregations, 2003 found Tim Owings re-inventing his professional life. Stepping away from two and a half decades of active pastoral work was not easy, but a new beginning was on the horizon. For the next three years, Mr. Owings worked as a financial stewardship consultant with RSI of Dallas, TX. In that role, he worked with congregations and non-profits across the country raising capital funds for building projects and ministry expansion. In 2007, he became a financial advisor with a national investment firm, obtaining the CERTIFIED FINANCIAL PLANNER™ designation in 2011. He holds FINRA Series 7 and 66 licenses, and the fixed and variable insurance and annuity licenses.

Having worked with men and women, families and business owners who face challenging personal problems, Tim offers a unique approach to helping clients with difficult life situations. He realizes he has a unique skill set that enables him to leverage his training and experience as a minister with the successful planning and practice management work done with clients. Writing to colleagues for his firm's intranet, he began to outline what is now *Cadence of Care: Imagining a Transformed Advisor-Client Experience*. The President of TL Owings & Associates, LLC, Tim actively manages his website, www.timowings.com. His current practice responsibilities limit regular speaking engagements, but for select finance and other care-centric professions, he occasionally offers highly-lauded seminars and keynote addresses.

A native of Miami, Florida, he graduated from Palm Beach Atlantic University and holds the M.Div. and Ph.D. in New Testament Literature from The Southern Baptist Theological Seminary in Louisville, Kentucky. Calling Augusta, Georgia home for over 26 years, he is a Sustaining Paul Harris Fellow of Rotary International and member of the Downtown Augusta Rotary Club. He is also a member and past President of Torch Club International of Augusta. Owings speaks in churches and other community gatherings on subjects ranging from grief recovery and embracing life's painful hurdles to making the most of your marriage and family. He continues his contributions to the life of the Christian community through his writing of homilies for GraceWorks Publishing.

Tim and his wife Kathie attend Reid Memorial Presbyterian Church. Devoted parents, they love spending time with their growing family: three adult children, their two beautiful daughters-in-law and five grandchildren. Among Tim's many interests, he enjoys in his spare time reading a good book, writing inspirational essays, and playing an occasional bridge game. He is a gifted teacher, writer, and student of the human experience. Virtuoso in music, he enjoys creating and performing piano arrangements. Each year during the Christmas season, Tim performs a popular Christmas concert at the piano for the Augusta community.

www.ingramcontent.com/pod-product-compliance
Lightning Source LLC
Chambersburg PA
CBHW070514200326
41519CB00013B/2802